A Dog in Hand

A Dog in Hand

TEACHING YOUR PUPPY TO THINK ...

BY GEORGE GATES, D.V.M.

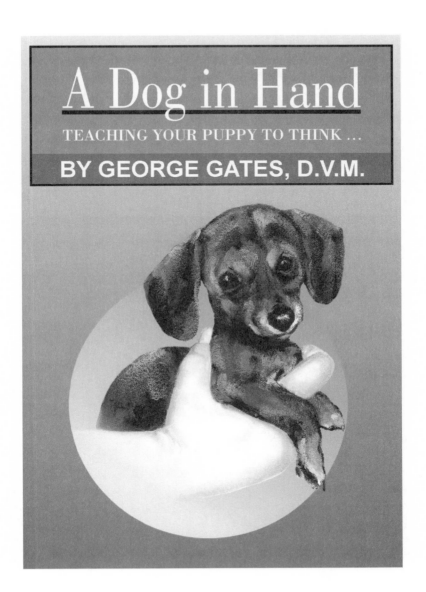

Tapestry Press
Irving, Texas

Tapestry Press
3649 Conflans Road
Suite 103
Irving, TX 75061

Printed in the U.S.A.
07 06 05 04 03 1 2 3 4 5

Library of Congress Cataloging-in-Publication Data
Gates, George, 1942-
    A dog in hand : teaching your puppy to think ... / by George
Gates.
        p. cm.
    ISBN 1-930819-28-5 (hard cover : alk. paper)
    1. Dogs--Training. 2. Dogs--Psychology. I. Title.
    SF431 .G37 2003
    636.7'0887--dc22

                                        2003014897

Cover design by Dennis Anderson
Illustrations by Dennis Anderson
Book design and layout by
D. & F. Scott Publishing, Inc.
N. Richland Hills, Texas

*Dedicated to my wife, Pam,
our three sons, Mike, John, and Jim,
and to those that have the will to parent*

Contents

Foreword

As a child psychologist with years of experience, I thought that I could handle our dog problems. Turned out I was wrong. When we had aggression problems with our two Jack Russells, my wife suggested that we schedule a "behavior" appointment with Dr. Gates. Reluctantly, I went just to satisfy her, not thinking that Dr. Gates would know what to do. Dr. Gates showed us what to do (firm pressure to calm their anxiety whenever one dog became aggressive toward the other), and the aggressive behavior stopped. We haven't had a problem with aggression since about one week after talking to Dr. Gates. Even Jack Russells can learn to control their anxiety.

There are literally millions of dog owners around the world, many starting out with a puppy. Over time, these dogs, if they are to coexist with their human owners, must be trained. For most of the time, owners just seem to survive instead of planning what they will do with their new friends. Issues such as getting your puppy to sleep through the night, housebreaking, and coming when called are often left up to chance and supplanted with an occasional swat with a hand or a newspaper. So many dog owners will then attribute their dog's bad habits to either breeding or a bad disposition.

Most owners, with little understanding of how and why their puppy is doing what she is doing, will rely on rewards like snacks and punishments like swats. Unfortunately, all that could have been gained by understanding what really makes dogs tick is usually just left by the wayside.

When a puppy whines its first night in your house, most dog owners will either take the dog into their bed, or they swat or yell at the puppy. These acts can create problems that may last a long, long time. It is better to understand that the dog is whining because he/she is anxious. Take a minute each time they whine to gently put pressure on their head and neck and reassure them that they are in an "okay" place and that they are going to be fine. My daughter talked to Dr. Gates about her new Boston terrier whining all night long. Calming her anxiety with the firm pressure took only a couple of days and it's no longer a problem.

George Gates knows a lot about dogs. He's helped thousands of dog owners learn to coexist with their dogs in a trusting, symbiotic relationship that is satisfying to both owner and dog. You have to read what he has to say, savor it, and understand what he is saying about your dog's needs. You may need to read what he has to say more than once, but once you understand it and can implement the procedures that he describes in the book, you will see that both you and your dog are much happier. Isn't that what having a dog is all about anyway?

Edward R. Christophersen, Ph.D., ABPP

Acknowledgments

I would like to thank Tom Stephenson for his patience and his help organizing my thoughts. This book would have never been completed without his help.

I would like to thank all of those who encouraged me to complete this project, including Dr. Ed Christophersen, my wife Pam and our sons, as well as my nephew Grant Hansen and his father Dale.

I would like to thank Dennis Anderson for the illustrations.

Finally, I would like to thank Bill Scott and Jill Bertolet of Tapestry Press for their assistance and counsel in all matters necessary to bring this book to print.

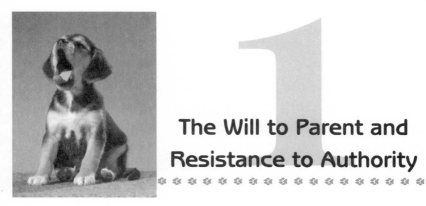

The Will to Parent and
Resistance to Authority

❈ ❈ ❈ ❈ ❈ ❈ ❈ ❈ ❈ ❈ ❈ ❈ ❈ ❈ ❈ ❈ ❈ ❈ ❈

I have been blessed with practicing a science and an art that I truly love and look forward to each day. In an average year I may handle or interact with three or four thousand individual dogs. Do that for more than thirty-five years and you have had a lot of social interactions with dogs. Since I have made my living touching and holding canine family members, I would like to present would-be puppy parents with a philosophy and technique that can place them in a unique position of using their hands and common sense to develop a relationship free of resistance. I am not trying to change the world; just offering some ideas that have worked for me and might help you develop a relationship of mutual trust, respect and self-control with your pet.

Today's puppy parents (the human kind) know less about animals than any previous generation in American history. Each generation is further removed from animal husbandry or animal agriculture—day to day working and living with animals. Urbanization has created a collision of man and beast that too often leaves a pet owner bewildered at the out-of-control behavior of his new canine companion. Millions of puppy parents begin their

1

journey naïve in the ways of the animal world and con-fused by conflicting advice from "experts." These new parents are ill-equipped to handle a dog's out-of-control anxiety or aggression.

It is instinctive for the youth of all species to resist authority or control, and it is no different with puppies. It becomes necessary to teach them trust and respect so that they can learn self-control. Teaching these lessons can be a tall order, because when you attempt to impose your will, their natural response is resistance or an at-tempt to escape. As a parent of both puppies and children, I have never learned how to totally avoid this difference of wills. However, when this occurs, you must have the will to control the outcome—to be the parent.

If you attempt to impose your will on a puppy, he will become anxious and attempt to escape your will. This anxiety is natural, but it must be calmed; uncontrolled anxiety is the root of almost all dog behavior problems. If the parent yields to the anxiety, the next time there is a dif-ference of wills, the anxiety will escalate and the puppy will continue to be out of control and will not learn self-con-trol. On the other hand, if the parent imposes his will in a firm yet gentle manner, the puppy will learn to control his anxiety and the desire to escape the control.

Many people also believe that the resistance mani-fested by aggression and even violence is a learned behavior. Consequently, when a person adopts a puppy that becomes dominant and aggressive, she assumes the puppy has been taught such behavior or that some-

thing terrible happened to the puppy before it was adopted. The parental instinct then is to relax their will and control. While I feel great empathy for these people, they could not be more wrong.

Simply *loving* and providing for his every *want* and *need* does not guarantee that a puppy will trust and respect your authority. Love and the willingness to respect and trust authority have little to do with each other in the dog's world. For example, you may believe that your dog loves you, but does he come when you call him, or when *he* wants to? Does he allow you to touch and hold him at times other than when *he* wants you to? Does he calm himself when you ask him to, or when *he* wants to?

Without a true understanding of dog behavior, people are more likely to have problems with their canine family members. Consequently, there is an increasingly greater need for people to have a *hands-on* relationship with their pet to acquire a true understanding of dog behavior.

Puppies will *not* exercise *self-control* until they have learned to trust and respect *parental* control or authority. The parenting methods I describe involve touching and holding your puppy with purpose, and that purpose is to teach your puppy to accept your physical control. If your puppy resists or wants to escape your controlling touches how do you achieve a relationship free of resistance? You must have the will to teach your puppy to control the anxiety associated with the resistance and once there is no anxiety there is no resistance. Remember, the anxiety associated with resistance is natural or instinctive while self control is a learned behavior.

Many training methods today encourage the use of positive reinforcement only. These methods are popular because they are said to be humane and non-abusive, and because they are thought to be easy. Let's face it, how tough is it to never say no? The easiest thing in the world is to say yes; there is never resistance to yes, while there is always resistance to no.

I had three different clients come to our clinic one day with puppies that were out of control. The clients had brought their pets for routine immunizations, and I asked them how they were getting along. All three had recently completed an obedience class, and when I asked what they had learned, they said they'd been taught to give treats to their dogs for good behavior and ignore the unwanted behavior. I explained that while food rewards were great to teach your puppy tricks, these "tricks" don't have much to do with a relationship of mutual trust and respect, not to mention self-control.

It has always amazed me that experts tell us to never confront unwanted behavior and to only use positive rein-forcement strategies. If a puppy is allowed to do any and every thing he wants to do and no one says no, how will he believe that any one cares what happens to him.

The same is true with humans: If no one says no and you feel that no one cares about you, how are you sup-posed to care about yourself or anyone else? For example, my parents didn't always allow me to do any and every

thing I wanted to do. I thought they were pretty "mean" at times, but there was never any question as to whether or not they cared about me or loved me. I learned that they valued my being alive and well. Consequently, I learned to value myself, or as it is said today, I developed self-esteem. I also learned that my parents knew more than I did. As my dad used to say, "Adults are supposed to have more sense than children." For the sake of this discussion, I would add, "People are supposed to have more sense than dogs."

There are no gimmicks here: The only way to teach a puppy that it is okay to be touched and held in a controlling manner is to touch and hold your puppy with that purpose in mind. You'll learn the meaning of a true attachment, a bond, to your dog. You'll learn the importance of teaching your puppy to think about someone other than herself. You'll learn that dogs can be taught to think and to be thoughtful and considerate of others. Dogs that are selfish and self-indulgent and inconsiderate are no different than people with the same attitude.

In this age that emphasizes "feel good" nurturing and avoiding confrontation, my philosophy may seem as old fashioned as my granddad's philosophy. He always told me a fellow could develop a bad habit in a day or two but it could take a lifetime to break the habit. How right he was.

Similarly, if a puppy gets into the habit of resisting and escaping control, it can become difficult to teach them to accept control as he matures. Consequently, I believe in the idea of teaching what is acceptable and what is not acceptable behavior very early in life.

In this book I refer to external control and self-control. The individual attempting to control or exercise authority is the external control, *the parent,* and the one that is being taught to accept control or authority, *the puppy,* is learning self-control.

For a puppy, one of the first lessons of life is to learn that it is okay to be *physically* controlled. Since dogs are so physical, parenting puppies must involve physically touching and holding them with purpose. The purpose is to teach them to think about how they behave, or self-control.

Most experts do not recommend having physical confrontations with your puppy. They believe that if you confront your puppy but fail to calm their anxiety and resistance to control, their out-of-control behavior will just be worse. Therefore, you're better off to not confront your puppy at all. The experts are right. However, I am confident that you can teach your puppy to control her anxiety and cause her to become a thoughtful and considerate member of your family—if you have the will.

Just as the youth of all species naturally resist control, their resistance can also be rather physical. How many times have you seen small children hit and kick their parents to resist control? Do you believe someone taught these children to hit and kick? I don't think so. Hitting and kicking is as natural for children as biting and scratching is for puppies. Some are just more inclined to be resistant than others

Many times puppies feel physically threatened even though no one lays a hand on them. For example, people

sometimes employ loud noises and sudden movements in an attempt to control their puppy's behavior. Such methods can cause puppies to feel physically threatened, resulting in anxiety and the impulse to escape. The methods I describe may cause a degree of anxiety, but you will be there to hold him through the anxious period and comfort him until the anxiety subsides. The method I describe prevents the puppy from getting into the habit of escaping or resisting the external control. Is my method physical? You bet. But this philosophy of dog parenting is more about *you* than the puppy.

Puppies are like children. Hold the smallest puppy against his will, and he'll squirm, cry and maybe bite. Such a puppy needs to learn right then not to resist your controlling touch. If you were holding your puppy at a busy intersection, you wouldn't let him down in traffic no matter how much he protested. But, you might let him down whenever he wanted if you were just sitting and watching TV.

What you need to realize is that your puppy's reason for wanting down is the same in both cases: He just wants down. It may be because he sees or hears or smells something that interests him. But it really should not matter why the puppy wants free from your control. In all cases, you are the external controller; it's your call whether he is allowed to get down, and not his.

Any time you ask a puppy to do something he doesn't want to do, there will be resistance that is manifested by escape behavior. Why does the puppy attempt to escape? Because he feels pressured or threatened in some way. It makes no difference whether the threat is real. It is the puppy's perception that counts, and that perception creates anxiety. If he is not able to relieve his anxiety by escaping the pressure, he may become aggressive. This is called the fight or flight response.

Think about the act of washing an infant's face. Not many babies that I know like to have their faces washed, but we do it anyway because we know we are not hurting them and they need to have their faces washed. After a while the baby learns that it is okay to have his face washed and there is less or no resistance. Can you imagine what it would be like to attempt to wash the face of a five or six year old that had never had his face washed?

So it is with puppies. It is instinctive for them to escape or resist the pressure of external control, while yielding to the pressure is a learned behavior. Yielding involves a thoughtful, decision-making process that will cause anxiety in the beginning. If the anxious puppy is allowed to escape the external control, future attempts to apply external control will create more anxiety and stress. On the other hand, if you teach your puppy to yield to the pressure and he gets through the anxiety, he is well on his way to becoming a thoughtful and considerate member of the family.

I once watched a real battle of wills outside my clinic window. Mom was attempting to strap a precious little two- or three-year-old-girl all dressed in pink and lace into a car seat. The little girl was more than a little resistant. The child arched her back then kicked and screamed, defying all

efforts at control. Mom was in there battling, holding the car seat down with her knee and calmly buckling the straps over the little girl whose face was now glowing a bright crimson. I thought right there: What a lesson! There is only one reason a resistant child is not strapped into a car seat. She must have a stronger will than the parent. Keep this example in mind as you read this book.

As you can see, it is very easy for puppies to get into the habit of doing everything and anything they want. They are very presumptuous and believe that everything they do is okay—and most of it *is*. Most dog behavior that people find objectionable is quite natural to the dog, and the qualities that are endearing are also quite natural. Let's face it, their natural curiosity and bumbling exuberant explorations are a large part of what makes them cute. Like my grandmother always said, "The only thing cuter than a puppy is two."

But they don't instinctively know which behaviors people like and which ones they dislike. We have to teach them, and there's a simple word for these teaching sessions. It's called parenting.

The biggest difference between a child and a puppy is that some day you will be able to sit down with the child and explain the virtues of behaving in a socially acceptable manner and hope that he will learn through his power of reasoning and not totally by experience. Not so with the puppy; he must learn by experience alone.

Back to my granddad: Another thing he used to tell me was that a fellow could get used to about anything. He was right again. Getting used to something is like getting into the habit of accepting something. Today we call it "becoming habituated." With diligent parenting, our puppies will make acceptable behavior a habit. If parenting begins early enough, they'll learn that making the right decision is not stressful at all.

If puppies are allowed to mature socially prior to being exposed to the stress of decision making, they can have a major panic episode when finally confronted. Remember that mother who was diligently strapping the defiant child into the car seat? Imagine what that confrontation would be like if the mother waited until her little girl was nine or ten years old.

The lesson here is that if we can couple emotional pressure with physical pressure early on, we can teach the puppy to control his anxiety. If we can reduce his level of anxiety, we can prevent a host of serious behavioral problems.

A good example can be seen when trying to trim a puppy's nails. Puppies do not like to have their feet controlled. If a puppy loses control of his feet, he becomes very vulnerable and puppies instinctively—and understandably—do not like to feel vulnerable. So if you attempt to control or hold a puppy's foot against his will, he will become anxious and the anxiety will cause him to resist or attempt to escape the physical control.

If you release your grasp of the puppy's feet as he pulls away, you are reinforcing his will to resist. On the other hand if you hold his foot firmly until he stops pulling away or resisting your control, he will learn that there is no reason for

anxiety; he will learn to trust the control and resist his instinct to escape. If done properly, the puppy learns that it is okay for you to control his foot and trim his nails. If on the other hand you let go of his foot every time he pulls away until he is five or six months old and *then* attempt to hold his foot against his will, your puppy will probably experience a major panic or anxiety attack.

A few years ago a client dropped off a fifty-pound puppy named Maggie for a nail trimming, saying she would be back to get Maggie in an hour. I had never met Maggie. When I reached to pet her, she was a little anxious. When I attempted to pick her up, she tried to bite me. I asked the attendant to leave Maggie alone and let me know when her owner returned. I wanted to talk to her about the dog's behavior.

Although Maggie was only five months old, she was very anxious. When her owner returned, I took Maggie into the examination room on a leash. When I asked the owner if she had been having any trouble with Maggie, she confirmed that she had. Maggie was out of control. She had been through obedience school and would heel on a leash. She would sit and stay for food rewards, which her owner was eager to show me. Maggie was sweet and loving as long as you touched her when and where she said it was okay.

But when Maggie was off the leash, no one could control her. And even on a leash she would only comply with your wishes if you didn't touch her. Her owner could pet and love Maggie when she said it was okay, but any effort to do something Maggie did not want to do was met with aggression.

I explained to the owner that I would be happy to trim Maggie's nails, but it was going to be very traumatic for the puppy—and maybe the owner too. I told her that Maggie was going to have a major panic attack because I was going to do something to her that no one had ever done in her short life. I was going to hold her when she resisted and keep holding her until she decided to relax.

Although physical restraint can be very stressful for a puppy, it is relatively easy to teach most puppies that it is okay to be restrained. Once puppies learn that it's okay to be physically controlled, they are capable of learning self-control and to think about what they do or how they behave.

For the first five months of her life, Maggie had never had anything done to her that she didn't like; she had never experienced controlling touches. I told the client I was going to bond with Maggie in a way she had never seen and that it would be physical for Maggie and for me. I told her that when I picked up Maggie, she was going to cry loudly as though she was in great pain, and I didn't want her to think I was abusing the dog. The client assured me that they were desperate—something had to be done if they were going to keep Maggie as a family pet.

When I reached down to pick up Maggie, she tried to bite me and yelped loudly. I grasped her firmly by the side of her head with one hand and placed my other hand under her belly. As she protested loudly, I picked her up and placed her on the exam table. I grasped her firmly behind

the ears, on each side of her neck, and held her as she cried and resisted violently. As I held her, I placed downward pressure on the back of her neck. Once she relaxed, I relaxed my grasp and praised her. I petted her for a while, then reached to pick up her foot. As I did so, she tried to bite me again. I grasped her firmly again and again she cried and resisted. Each time she tried to bite me, I held her firmly by the neck and applied pressure until she relaxed. The hold I used is not a choking hold but rather is similar to the head catch of a squeeze chute for cattle or head restraint bars. There is no pressure unless there is resistance. Once the resistance stops, the pressure stops.

After the third episode, I reached down to hold her front paw and she began licking my hand, and as I praised her she started licking my face and wagging her tail. Then I trimmed her nails without incident.

The client was incredulous. "I can't believe it! I can't believe it!" she cried.

"Can't believe what?" I asked.

"You made more progress in twenty minutes than we made in four weeks working with an animal behaviorist," she said. I told her that Maggie was capable of becoming a fine family pet if they would hold and touch Maggie, and bond with the dog as the authorities.

I asked the client to place her hands on the top of Maggie's head and press down with gentle but firm pressure. Each time she did so, Maggie responded with less resistance and eventually became quite affectionate. I then had the client touch Maggie all over her body, including her feet.

Five years later, I still see Maggie. She has become a wonderful family member. In fact, the client tells me Maggie is the best dog they've ever had.

Fortunately, Maggie was only five months old when she came to our clinic. Had she been older, the process would have been much more difficult and more dangerous. If the bonding process had started when Maggie was eight weeks old, I'm sure the problem would never have developed.

It is very common for people to not have a major problem until the puppy is older, when at two to three years old they suddenly want to establish control or teach their puppy self-control. By that age, the dog has been *top dog* for some time and is unwilling to relinquish his status for a few treats. In fact, in almost every case of a "problem dog," that reversal of roles is the cause. Once a puppy has established control of your house, it can be very stressful for everyone if you attempt to reverse the roles. In most cases, the reality is that once the dog has gained control, the people just learn how to live with a dog that has the upper hand in the relationship.

The key to the parenting process is to teach your puppy to think about what he does. He knows instinctively what is easy and what is difficult, so as a puppy parent your job is to make the right choice easy and the wrong choice difficult, and before you know it there will be no wrong choices.

Learning from Consequences

❀ ❀

I n nature, even the most primitive animals learn to control their instincts and urges to some extent. Wild predators are very capable of killing each other, but they learn to control their aggression toward each other. Unfortunately, the same cannot always be said for humans. That is why I believe that domestic dogs are more like people than their distant relatives, the wolves. Wolves rarely kill each other, but dogs and humans kill each other every day. Wolves rarely kill wantonly; dogs and people do.

I will never forget coming home with the family from church one Sunday as a child and finding a hundred dead chickens strewn over the barnyard. "Some wild animal must have killed all of our chickens," I said to my dad.

My dad answered sternly: "No wild animal would kill a hundred chickens and leave them lay! Only a dog or person would do a thing like this." About that time, we saw a stray dog chasing the one remaining chicken around the corner of the chicken house.

Since dogs are capable of killing each other, it becomes important for them to learn to control their aggression. In fact, the only behavior that I have seen a mother dog not tolerate is out-of-control aggression. If a puppy allows his aggression to get out-of-control, the mother will deliver an immediate negative consequence.

Puppies are very physical by nature and engage in activities that are rather rowdy and aggressive. For example, they play keep away, hide and seek, tug of war, and king of the mountain. They sneak-attack each other from the rear and the flank, as well as conduct head-to-head and paw-to-paw combat. They wrestle and tumble for hours. When puppies are not sleeping or eating they are usually play-fighting.

It is interesting to watch puppies interact. They are constantly competing for "top dog" status by literally trying to get on top of each other. Most puppies don't make a big deal out of having another pup on top, because in the next round he may be the one on top. However, some puppies never want to be the "under dog," and if another puppy tries to get on top, he may become aggressive. If the aggression becomes out-of-control, the mother will intervene by applying an immediate negative consequence.

Puppies not only interact with their siblings; they also interact with their mother. They attack her around the head and neck, grab her ears and lips, and pounce playfully on her tail. They sometimes can even become aggressive while they are nursing. As long as the aggression is controlled and no one gets hurt, the mother is very tolerant. However, if the aggression becomes out-of-control, the mother applies an immediate negative consequence.

You must remember that dogs do not think in terms of punishment and reward, but in terms of *immediate* negative and positive consequences. How do I know this? No one can say with certainty what a dog is actually thinking. However, we can interpret what we believe he is thinking by the way he acts.

When you watch animals interact, there is no question that they learn by experiencing immediate consequences. For example, a puppy might become out-of-control when interacting with his mother. If he bites her ear too hard and causes her pain, she will immediately grasp him by the back of the neck, apply downward pressure and hold him down until he calms himself. Sometimes the mother places her paw on the puppy and holds him down.

If a puppy nurses too aggressively, the mother reacts immediately and applies pressure. She does not go after her babies as though she were killing snakes; she merely applies sufficient pressure to stop the unwanted behavior. Once the puppy yields to the mother's control, they show each other what we would call affection. There is no harm to the pup—but neither is there escaping the negative consequences of unwanted behavior.

The application of the negative consequence is controlled. The mother is not telling them they cannot nurse or play with her. She is merely telling them to be more thoughtful and considerate next time. We know that the puppies do not fear their mother because they continue to nurse and interact with her, but they also think twice before they get out-of-control again. In human terms, we would call the relationship "respectful."

I like to compare the mouth of a mother dog to the human hand. The mother dog is capable of using her mouth to kill prey. She can also use her mouth to apply firm pressure to her babies when necessary, as well as apply soothing and gentle touches. Each act requires self-control. The same can be said for the hand of mankind.

While puppies learn from their mother how to behave in the canine world, they'll never learn from her how to be thoughtful and considerate members of the human family. They can only learn what people expect of them by interacting with people. Consequently it is necessary for the human parents to do some further teaching—further parenting. I don't know of a better way to teach a puppy right from wrong than to pick up right where the mother left off.

It is important to understand that everything puppies do that aggravates or irritates us comes very naturally to them. Puppies do not chew and jump on us to aggravate us; they do not knock over vases or tear up sofa cushions or pee on oriental carpets just to make us unhappy. They don't bark and chase madly around just to annoy us. They do these things because they are what dogs do. It is therefore necessary to teach puppies to control their urges and instincts if we want a desirable relationship in an environment where most of the furnishings and the general household peace remain intact.

Puppies learn what is not wanted by receiving an immediate negative consequence, and they learn what is wanted by receiving an immediate positive consequence. A basic law of nature tells us that immediate negative consequences reduce the chances that a behavior will be repeated and immediate positive consequences increase the chances that a behavior will be repeated. You do not need to sit down and explain or plead with a puppy about the ethical niceties of what is right and what is wrong. It is sufficient for them to know instinctively the difference between an immediate negative consequence, which is uncomfortable and unpleasant, and an immediate positive consequence, which is comfortable and pleasing.

Mother dogs don't go into great philosophical detail about why they apply a negative consequence for unwanted behavior. They just do it. The negative consequence is immediate and nothing more than firm physical pressure. The positive consequence is the lack of physical pressure and the return of normal relations.

The art of parenting involves developing the skill to teach the puppy to yield to the pressure or control rather than allowing his instinct to resist and escape the pres-

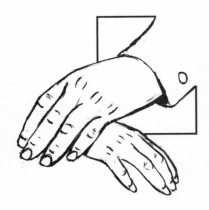

This hand-on-hand demonstration gives an idea of the difference in feel between resistance and yielding to pressure. Remember, the pressure or control is passive—no resistance, no pressure.

sure to prevail. To physically demonstrate the principal of yielding versus resisting, I will often ask the puppy parent to place her hand on the examination table palm down. While the parent's hand is in that position, I gently place my hand on top of the parent's hand, palm down (see illustration). The upper hand represents the external control (parent), while the hand underneath represents self-control (puppy). I then ask the client to resist the external control by lifting her hand. As she does so, I hold my hand more firmly in place, preventing the client from lifting hers with a pressure that is equal only to her resistance.

The more strenuously the client resists the firm pressure, the more firmly but equally I apply the counter-resistance. I then ask the client to relax. The instant she relaxes, there is no pressure. I then ask the client who controls the amount of pressure that is received. Most say the person whose hand is on top, but they are wrong.

When a puppy feels pressure, his instincts cause him to become anxious and he continues to resist or attempt to escape. However, if the pressure is sustained until the puppy relaxes, he learns to trust and respect the external control. When the puppy learns to control his anxiety and to trust and respect the external authority, he has learned to exercise self-control. Self-control is a learned behavior that allows the individual to control the degree of pressure he receives when the external control is passive. Passive control or pressure allows the student to learn the difference between a resistant and a resistant-free relationship. In my experience the student, when given a choice, will chose a relationship free of resistance. There is only one catch; the parent must have the will to sustain the pressure anytime there is resistance and maintain the pressure until the puppy calms himself.

Unfortunately, it is difficult for some people to differentiate between asking and forcing the puppy to yield to pressure. Many times when I demonstrate the hand-on-hand technique, people say, "You are *forcing* me to relax." I prefer to call the application of pressure during resistance a "firm insistence." Without a firm insistence, there is no progress—just continued resistance. Forcing does not give the puppy an opportunity to make a decision to yield, because the pressure is continuous regardless of the puppy's decision. However, by preventing the hand from escaping, I am asking or insisting that the person make a decision to relax. It is *their* choice.

If we understand that resisting control is instinctive and yielding to control is learned behavior, we are well on our way to understanding how dogs think. Dogs instinctively know the difference between a positive, pleasing consequence and a negative, unpleasant consequence. This is the basic principle that teaches the puppy to think.

One of the most important things for the parent to understand is that at first there is always an effort to escape or resist the pressure (control), because puppies are anxious creatures by nature, and some are more anxious than others. If the puppy is not allowed to escape, he will become even more anxious. However, if the puppy is released every time he becomes anxious, he will never learn to control his anxiety. Instead, he'll associate escape with the relief of his anxiety. What the parent must do is continue to hold the puppy until the anxiety is gone and the puppy relaxes. Only then will he learn the positive consequences of self-control.

An interesting example of this is Aunt Millie and her dog Trixie.

Trixie was three years old and had never bitten anyone until one day when he rather viciously attacked Aunt Millie's three-year-old nephew as he carried a rolled newspaper to her. When the attack occurred, Aunt Millie thought that the little boy must have abused Trixie with the newspaper. Otherwise, why would the dog do such a horrible thing? If it wasn't her nephew, it must have been some other child.

I had a difficult time convincing Aunt Millie that no child had abused Trixie. She had owned Trixie since he was eight weeks old and thought she had the dog under her control because she could stop him from doing things she didn't want him to do. For example, if Trixie were chewing on her favorite Oriental rug, she would stop him by pounding a rolled newspaper against the table or counter and yelling at him. While the loud noise was effective in stopping the unwanted behavior, if Aunt Millie wanted to pick Trixie up immediately after scolding him, he would escape behind the couch. And if she tried to pick him up while he was hiding there, he would growl and threaten to bite her. Aunt Millie was smart enough to know better than to force the issue and would leave Trixie alone. She knew he was sorry for the way he behaved, because after a while he would come out from behind the couch and crawl up onto her lap and "beg forgiveness."

Though Aunt Millie was convinced she was in control, there was no question in Trixie's mind who was really in control. Top dogs are only touched when and where they say it is okay, and Aunt Millie was never allowed to touch Trixie except when he indicated it was okay.

Because Trixie had never experienced control, he had not learned self-control. As he matured socially, he became more assertive and more anxious. When the little boy walked directly toward Aunt Millie carrying the newspaper, Trixie felt threatened, which typically triggers one of two instinctive reactions: flight or fight. In this case, he chose the latter and attacked. I can't say with absolute certainty what Trixie was thinking, but I know how he acted. Realistically, I don't think Trixie was thinking at all, because Aunt Millie had never taught him to be thoughtful and considerate.

People often tell me that their puppy "sasses" them. I tell them that if they do not scold their puppy, he will not sass them. Many dogs that become "problem dogs" as they mature have a history of being scolded in an effort to stop unwanted behavior. A puppy may tolerate being scolded until he becomes socially mature. Then, the dog perceives the scolding as a threat and may become aggressive.

To calm large breed puppies, drop to your knees and wrap your arms around them and hold them against your chest with firm pressure until they are calm. Say *no* to the excited or anxious behavior and *yes* to the calm behavior.

I am not sure why but people will go to great lengths to avoid touching their dog during an encounter or confrontation. I have had no choice but to touch and hold puppies in a controlling manner if I am to do my job. I have become habituated to holding puppies, many times against their will, and it is difficult for me to understand why people are so resistant to holding their puppy with the purpose of teaching self-control.

In my veterinary practice I have the opportunity to follow up and see how my patients are doing over long spans of time. It is not unusual for people with new puppies to encounter problems two to four years down the road. As some dogs mature they become more and more anxious. One client had a four-year-old dog named Missy that was becoming increasingly anxious when people came to the door. In fact, Missy was becoming more anxious each time she came to the clinic. On one particular day Missy barked at me when I entered the exam room. As she barked at me, the parent applied positive consequences by petting her and saying, "It's okay, it's okay." However, when I looked at Missy and she growled, the parent placed her hands on Missy and said "no" as she applied pressure. Missy stopped her aggressive behavior immediately. The parent said, "I should have calmed her when she was barking rather than praising her by telling her it was okay, right?" I agreed and explained that she should use her hands to calm Missy when people come to the door. Fortunately, the parents had worked with Missy when she was a puppy and had held her in a controlling manner and had taught her to calm herself. All that was needed was to give Missy a refresher course in self-calming and she is doing fine. It is important to recognize and anticipate anxious behavior so that you can insist that the puppy calm himself immediately. By doing so, you can prevent some bad habits from forming.

Not all of my clients buy into my ideas on teaching dogs to think and to control their anxiety and aggression. Sam was a nice young man who was proud of his new friend Rambo. In fact, as he put Rambo on the table in my examining room, Sam remarked: "Hey Doc, what do you think of this little fellow? I picked him because he has an attitude."

Rambo was eight weeks old, and when I examined him I agreed with Sam that Rambo had an attitude. He resisted being held and examined. That's not unusual; many puppies resist being touched in a controlling manner, but they usually calm themselves after a moment or two.

Calm behavior is important when examining puppies and dogs. For example, to listen to a puppy's heart with a stethoscope, the puppy must hold still. When you place your hands and the stethoscope on the puppy, they are often very quiet at first but may start wiggling and squirming to get away from your grasp. All that is needed in most cases is to passively hold the puppy until he stops resisting.

I tried this with Rambo, and he continued to resist. I told Sam he should be firm and insist that Rambo calm himself, but Sam refused to have anything to do with that approach. Apparently, it wasn't "modern" enough for him; he said he was going to parent Rambo using only positive reinforcement. I explained that he needed to teach him right from wrong using immediate consequences, positive and negative.

Sam said my methods were too "physical," and he didn't want to be physical with his new friend. That's not an unusual reaction from pet owners. If you are holding a puppy passively and he starts to cry and wiggle, the client many times will think that the puppy is being hurt physically. Although I understand their feeling, they need to understand that it is normal for puppies to cry when they don't get their way.

Still, Sam wanted to treat Rambo in a nonphysical manner, and Rambo soon proved that he did not share Sam's delicate sensitivities. On a later visit, Sam said that Rambo had refused to get off the bed one night, and when Sam reached for him, Rambo growled. Sam lured him off the bed with food. By this time, Rambo weighed eighty pounds and was without a doubt the "top dog" of the house. Sam was the one paying the mortgage, and the bank still held the papers, but it was clear that Rambo considered himself the rightful owner.

Since Sam had handed control of the relationship to Rambo, I explained to him that he needed to be careful and should never do anything that Rambo would interpret as a gesture to physically control him. If he did, his perceived threat could cause Rambo to become very aggressive.

Sam muddled along under the Rambo Regime for six months until one night when Rambo reacted just as I had warned. Rambo was lying on the floor between Sam and the telephone. When the phone rang, Sam stepped over

Rambo to get it. However, his foot slipped and he did a spread eagle on top of Rambo. His leg grazed the back of the dog's neck, and Rambo reached up and sank his teeth deep into Sam's thigh.

Sam came to me a few days later wanting to know why and how Rambo could do such a horrible thing. I explained that the pressure placed on the back of Rambo's neck was perceived as a physical threat to his top dog status and he reacted instinctively. Rambo had not been habituated to controlling touches and had not learned to trust and respect external control or authority. As a result, he had not learned self-control. Sam had no idea that a dog could become so aggressive without being taught such behavior. He did not understand that aggressive behavior is natural or instinctive, and the control of aggression is a learned behavior.

I'll never forget another day when a young woman with a three-pound dog came to my office crying because her dog had bitten the end of her finger. She was not crying because of physical pain; she was crying because her feelings were hurt.

"I know dogs love me because I love all dogs," she said. "They know I love them. Why would my own dog bite me?" Sure, she loved her dog, and the dog probably loved her. But she forgot—or did not know how—to teach him trust, respect and self-control.

If you believe dogs learn from immediate consequences, you must be willing to apply the negative consequence, and the negative consequence needs to be nothing more than firm pressure applied with your hands. By doing so you teach the puppy that his cue for calm relaxed behavior is your hand. By teaching him to accept your external control, he learns self-control.

As much as this all makes sense, many pet owners still have difficulty applying this firm pressure. They do not have the will to hold on long enough for the puppy to get through the anxiety and calm himself. The puppy expresses discomfort with the pressure of external control, and the owner does not want to be the "bad guy," so they yield to the puppy. In the short term, everybody feels good, but over the long haul, damage is done.

Calming the Anxiety

❋ ❋ ❋ ❋ ❋ ❋ ❋ ❋ ❋ ❋ ❋ ❋ ❋ ❋ ❋ ❋ ❋ ❋ ❋

There is no getting around it: Puppies are anxious, eager, skittish creatures, and some are more anxious than others. Puppies are easily overstimulated, and when they become overstimulated they become out of control. In essence, the environment has taken over control of them. Puppies are also multi-sensory stimulated. They have a range of senses we can only *imagine*. They react to all sorts of sights and sounds as well as different odors, changes in their daily routine or changes in the location of objects in their environment. They can detect sounds far beyond the range of our hearing, they can detect the slightest movement, and they can readily smell a number of things we'd probably just as soon not. Dogs are constantly being accused of sounding false alarms. The alarm is not false; the stimuli that causes the response is beyond our sensory capability. If you pay attention to your dog, you can become much more aware of *your* environment.

Having these keen senses helps with survival, but in some cases they also make puppy parenting rather difficult. Puppies are much like children that are said to have attention deficit disorder. They are very easily distracted and it is hard for them to focus on the parent or teacher.

As a veterinarian who has made his living touching and holding dogs, I have seen lots of anxious dogs, and it is interesting to see how differently people attempt to calm them.

A few years back, a client brought her new puppy for his initial check-up. I had known the client for thirty years, and this was the third dog for which I had provided care.

This puppy was different from the previous two that she had adopted. He was very anxious and out of control. During the short visit, the client asked her new friend to "calm down" at least a hundred times.

"Sit still!" she'd also say, but the puppy kept squirming and goofing around. "Behave!" she'd try, but the dog would obliviously pay her no mind and go about its business—or monkey business. But her main command was "calm down," so while she was telling me how "different and remarkable" this puppy was, I grabbed a felt-tip marker and wrote in bold letters on a large piece of paper, "CALM DOWN." Then I held the paper in front of the puppy's face so he could see it. The "different and remarkable" puppy just looked at it.

The client, curious, took the paper and examined it for a long moment, puzzled over it about as much as the puppy had, and then exclaimed, "George, what did you do that for? You know she can't read."

Then the lady "got it." She started laughing and agreed that not only can puppies not read but they also don't understand English very well.

Puppies are very capable of learning a spoken language, but it is essential to show them what you are asking. If you want your puppy to get in his bed, take him to his sleeping area and tell him that is his bed. Do this a few times and he will learn what the words mean and he will go to his bed when you ask.

Budding would-be novelists are told that they should "show, not tell." That same advice applies double to anyone who would parent a pup. Sometimes I have a client who takes this advice to heart.

I had been taking care of Brandy since she was a pup, and she was becoming more and more anxious with age. When Brandy was twelve, the client brought her in for an examination, and she was even more anxious than usual. She was panting and pacing on the exam table. Her eyes were dilated and her heart was beating faster than normal.

As I was about to explain to the client that it was okay and I was used to anxious patients, he grasped her with both hands and pressed her firmly against his chest and at the same time said in a firm voice, "Brandy, calm yourself." I stood there in amazement as Brandy relaxed, her heart rate slowed to normal and she quit panting and her eyes became less dilated. I asked the client, "Where did you learn how to do that?" He said, "Learn what? It is just what *you* do, isn't it?" I responded, "Yes sir!"

He'd been watching what I'd shown Brandy on past visits. At home he'd been showing her— rather than just "telling" her. And she'd gotten it. In fact, when the dog was at home, the words alone were usually enough; but in the excitement of the trip to the vet's office, they required some "refresher" physical reinforcement; some "show and tell."

These examples of two different attempts to calm a puppy "show" us mainly this: One method works, and the other doesn't.

After I'd played my little "flash card" joke on the client who asked her dog to "calm down," I told her that if she wanted her new friend to calm down, she should hold her firmly until she was calm, then praise the calm behavior. She tried it and after a few minutes and some firm holding, the puppy was calm and relaxed. I explained that this puppy was more sensitive and more easily overstimulated than her previous puppies. As a consequence, she would require a parent willing to impose her will *with sufficient strength and firmness to calm the anxiety yet gentle enough to comfort.*

What Makes the Best Dog?

Early in my career I was associated with a veterinarian who would always recommend that people get a puppy from a family with several small children. His thought was that a puppy that grew up with children would be well socialized and easy to live with. He was absolutely correct. Not only are such puppies well socialized but they've also learned self-control.

When I tell people that the best dogs in the world are dogs that have grown up in the hands of small children, they look at me like I am crazy. But, the simple fact is that children do not mind imposing their will upon a puppy (or their parents for that matter). If a puppy doesn't want to be held, the kids don't care. They hold him anyway.

Watch a four- or five-year-old child hold a puppy. If the puppy squirms and wiggles, the child will hold tighter (unless the parents interfere). The more the puppy wiggles, the tighter the child will hold on until the puppy relaxes. Once the puppy relaxes, the child relaxes his hold and can carry the puppy around like a sack of potatoes. The puppy gets into the habit of not resisting or escaping the control. The child has taught the puppy, in the phrase popularized by a 1990s TV space opera, that "resistance is futile."

Yet in all my years of practice, I have never seen a puppy injured as a result of a small child holding too firmly. On the other hand, I have seen many puppies injured as a result of adults not holding firmly enough and allowing the puppy to jump out of their arms. I have seen broken necks, broken legs, internal injuries and concussions as a result of adults not willing to impose their will upon a puppy.

All Puppies Are Different

Keep in mind, though, that all puppies are not born equal, at least in terms of "the will to resist"—not even in the same litter. It is very interesting to go through a litter of puppies and pick each one up and hold it. I am talking about two-, three- or four-week-old puppies. Each one will have a different feel. For example, one puppy may become rigid and stiff when picked up, yet his littermate may be completely relaxed. The puppy that becomes anxious when picked up will soon overcome his anxiety if he is picked up and held often enough. He will become habituated.

Unfortunately, the puppy that is resistant to being held is the one that needs it the most and will likely be the one that gets held the least. Why? Because people are reluctant to impose their will upon a puppy. They think that if the puppy doesn't want to be held, then they shouldn't hold him.

In this chapter, I am going to show you how to anticipate anxious and resistant behavior and how to deal with it and prevent serious behavior problems. The emphasis will be on using your hands with a sensible purpose to touch and hold your puppies and build the confident two-way relationship we are all so desperately seeking.

Calming Exercises

It is difficult for most people to understand how simply holding and touching a puppy with purpose can help calm his anxiety, teach self-control, and develop a relationship of mutual trust and respect.

First of all, holding a puppy with purpose is not as simple as it sounds. You ask, "What's the big deal about holding my puppy? He loves to be held and I hold him all the time." The key word is "purpose," and the purpose is to hold your puppy in a way that teaches trust, respect, and self-control.

Such an effort requires the parent to hold his puppy in a way he does not always like, even if he resists. And what he does like at one age may create anxiety at another. For example, if you hold a six-week-old puppy in your arms with his head resting on your forearm and his front feet under your forearm while his body is cradled

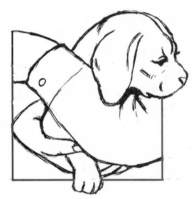

Holding your puppy with your fore-arm between his feet and head can cause him to become anxious. However, if your puppy will allow you to hold him in this manner, he will learn to trust your control.

Puppies prefer not to have their feet and head controlled. However, when puppies are held in this manner, it is easy for them to resist and escape your control. First they must learn to accept physical control.

with the other arm, he may not resist at all (see illustrations). Try this same hold a few weeks later and you could have your hands full. That's because as puppies mature, they like to place their feet and their head where they want them. When puppies lose control of their feet and head, they become vulnerable and they resist this loss of control. Once they learn that no harm will come, they learn to trust and respect control.

Anxiety Increases with Maturity

It is not uncommon for people to encounter aggressive behavior from their puppy as he matures, such as when they attempt to move him from their lap or from the couch. A client, Mrs. Wills, once came to me very upset because her two-year-old puppy had bitten her on the cheek. I had taken care of Fifi since she was eight weeks old and I knew she was top dog at their house. I told Mrs. Wills that Fifi bit her on the cheek because she had unknowingly challenged Fifi's top dog status. Mrs. Wills had always allowed Fifi to climb up onto her shoulder and place her head where she wanted to. This time, however, in an effort to show Fifi affection, Mrs. Wills had placed her head on top of Fifi's while Fifi's head was on her shoulder. Fifi interpreted this gesture of affection as a threat to her top dog status, and since she had been top dog for two years, she saw no reason to relinquish her status now. Mrs. Wills was okay with the explanation because she knew Fifi was top dog, but she wanted to know why Fifi waited two years to display her aggression.

I can only speculate, but I believe it took Fifi two years to establish her status, and once she was confident her status was secure, she became aggressive when she felt challenged. It is not an unusual occurrence for dogs to wait until they are two, three, or four years old to display aggressive behavior. Only Fifi knows for sure. I can say one thing with certainty, and that is that if Mrs. Wills had habituated Fifi to controlling touches, Fifi would not have reacted the way she did. Placing your hand or head on top of a dog's head is a controlling touch, and controlling touches cause anxiety unless the puppy has learned to accept control.

Puppies like to get up on top. They like to be "top dog." When you are holding your puppy in your arms, he will most likely tolerate being held with his head and feet resting on top of your shoulder. If your puppy is the least bit anxious by nature and something happens to make him feel threatened, he will climb up as high as he can get on your shoulder or possibly your head. If you allow your puppy to escape the perceived threat by climbing all over you, he is not learning to control his anxiety. On the other hand, if you hold him firmly, preventing his escape, and say the word *no*, he will soon give up the idea of escaping and calm himself.

Puppies prefer to place their feet on top. When a puppy becomes anxious, he will climb higher.

If your puppy is extremely anxious and you don't allow him to climb up on you, he might become aggressive. He might cry and bite. If he does, just hold him until he stops because if you let go and make a half-hearted attempt to control him, you are making matters worse.

Calm the Anxiety First

I cannot overemphasize how important it is for the puppy parent to hold with sufficient firmness to calm the anxiety yet be gentle enough to comfort. But you must calm the anxiety *first*. If you do not calm the anxiety or cause the puppy to calm himself prior to releasing him, you are fostering resistant or escaping behavior.

I was showing a client how to hold a puppy with purpose one day, and things went pretty good until the puppy heard a noise and wanted down right away. The puppy squirmed and cried as I held her, but in a few seconds, she forgot about whatever it was that stimulated her in the first place and calmly focused on me.

The client asked, "How can you be so sure you are not hurting the puppy when she cries out like that?" My response: "Common sense and a lot of years of touching and holding puppies." The client went on to say she would be the first one to let go if she had not seen how the puppy calmed herself so quickly.

I know that it is not always easy to impose your will upon a puppy, but as a veterinarian there have been many times when I have had no choice but to hold a puppy against his will to do my job.

In the days when parvovirus infection was epidemic, sometimes whole litters would become infected. Infected puppies became very ill and intensive care was a must. Puppies had to be given intravenous fluids, medications, and constant nursing; sometimes they spent as much as three weeks in the hospital. Those puppies that survived were almost always super dogs, behavior-wise.

People were always amazed at how happy the puppies were to come back for their re-checks, particularly after all these puppies had been through. The clients would think the puppies were grateful to us because we saved their life. I always thought it was because they were in the hospital so long and had everything done to them. Consequently, they became habituated. Like my granddaddy told me, "A fellow can get used to about anything." In the case of these puppies, a true and firm bond had been formed.

Look at it this way: If you knew someone who could invariably help you calm yourself at those times when you became overwrought, overstimulated and extremely anxious, wouldn't you consider that person your friend?

Use Your Hands to Lay the Puppy Down

A simple little exercise that helps puppies learn to control their anxiety involves placing both hands on the back of the puppy's neck and head and asking them to lay down as pressure is applied. If it is a small-breed puppy, I like to lay them down on a table or counter-top. With larger breeds I get down on the floor with them.

Using your hands to lay your puppy down teaches him to trust and respect your hands. The hand that applies the pressure is the same hand that applies the gentle touches.

I work with the puppy using my hands until I have him on his chest and his head resting on the same level as his body (see illustration). I might work his front feet forward and work his back feet up under his body, while at all times applying slight pressure. Once he is lying down and somewhat relaxed, there is no pressure. If the puppy attempts to get up before he is asked to get up, I say the word "stay" and hold him with firm pressure until he yields to the pressure and relaxes. I keep doing this exercise until the puppy yields to the slightest pressure without resistance. By repeating this exercise, I am teaching him that his cue for calm *and relaxed* behavior is my hand.

I recommend that people lay their puppy down two to three times a day for five to ten minutes and continue this routine throughout his first two to three years. Lying your puppy on his sternum with his head resting on the same surface as his feet places him in the most vulnerable position possible. Being vulnerable without being harmed teaches trust.

"Submissive" Puppies

Some puppies like to roll over onto their back or side when efforts are made to lay them down. Many people feel that the puppy is assuming a "submissive posture." It may be a submissive posture, but it is also a "defensive" posture. If the puppy attempts to roll onto his back or side, don't let him, because he feels threatened and feels a need to defend himself. We can increase the puppy's confidence if we prevent him from assuming this defensive posture. When he is in the truly vulnerable position and no harm comes to him, he will learn to trust. A trusting puppy is much more fun to live with than one that lacks confidence and feels threatened.

Children and Anxious Puppies

One of the most difficult tasks of a puppy parent is protecting small children from overly excited puppies. Dogs in general like to go after anything that moves and makes noise—especially high-pitched noise. Small children fulfill this criterion. Some of our younger readers may not remember the Coppertone ad that shows a puppy pulling the swimsuit bottom off a small child. The ad was very cute and amusing to the viewing public, but I doubt that the small child thought it was very amusing.

Puppy teeth are very sharp and can cause children pain. I have seen small children run and scream at the site of a puppy. Naturally the puppy goes after the child if not supervised. A parent once told me her puppy bit her small child on the ankle but it was not the dog's fault because her child was kicking the puppy. The most common cause for a child to kick a puppy is when the puppy has chased the child and has him cornered. The child cannot escape the threat and, in an effort to protect, he starts kicking his feet (fight or flight). The feet are harmlessly flying through the air, but the movement excites the puppy that much more and he engages in aggressive play.

In such cases, I suggest the puppy parent take hold of the leash (which should be on the puppy) and bring the puppy close and hold him to calm him down. The parent might want to calm the child down also. The best thing to do is not allow such things to happen in the first place, but that is a bit idealistic.

Another situation that causes a problem with children and puppies, as well as adults, is when the person reaches out to pet the puppy and the puppy starts chewing on the hand. The person pulls the hand back and reaches again, and again the puppy "playfully" attacks the hand. The moving hand is a stimulus, and the puppy will go after the hand as though it were a littermate. Surely you have seen how puppies chew on each other?

All that is needed is to hold the puppy's head firmly and say *no* and continue to hold the puppy until he stops. If he continues to chew on your hands, you are not insistent enough.

Head in the Hand Exercise

Another good exercise is to hold the puppy's head in your hands and have the child reach out and pet the puppy on top of the head repeatedly. If the puppy attempts to chew on the child's hand, hold the puppy's head so that he can't.

I cannot overemphasize how important it is for the parent to be firm and insistent in order to achieve the desired result—total trust and relaxation. If there is resistance or a continued effort to escape, you are doing something wrong. Perhaps in past attempts you have given up too soon. If you attempt to use your hands to calm your puppy and you do not persevere until you are successful, you are making things worse. You are reassuring your puppy that it's okay for his emotional "escape" reactions to take over, and that there is no need for self-control. The idea is to keep your hands on the puppy through the anxious period and continue holding through the calming period.

I often hear dog trainers tell people to not apply pressure to the dog's back when they are teaching them to sit because they resist pressure. They are absolutely correct: Dogs do resist pressure because it is instinctive—but it is my firm opinion that dogs must learn to yield to pressure rather than resist. Resisting pressure is natural, while yielding to pressure is a learned behavior. Teaching puppies to yield to pressure is the basis for establishing a strong bond and a resistance-free relationship.

A dog may provide an indicator of his level of trust when you reach out to pet him on top of the head. If the dog lowers his head and half closes his eyes, many people think the dog is cringing because he has been beaten and abused. When I raise my hand and a dog lowers his head and squints a little, I know he trusts me and it is okay to touch him on top of the head. If on the other hand he raises his head and his eyes dilate, I know he does not trust me at that particular moment. However, if I work with him for a few moments, there is a good chance he will learn to trust me.

Think about it: If someone you don't know or trust reaches to touch you on top of the head, you will raise your head and watch the hand very closely with wide eyes, and if the person pressures you, you will back up. If you really don't want to be touched and become cornered, you might become aggressive. On the other hand, if you trust the person and know they would never harm you, there is no need for anxiety and you might lower your head and allow the person to touch you.

Another exercise that is helpful in developing a resistant-free relationship is the "hand on top of the head" exercise. While you are holding your puppy or laying him down, place your hand on top of his head and the back of his neck. Apply slight pressure if he resists and hold until he relaxes. You will be able to feel him relax. Once you feel the slightest yield, release the pressure. Keep doing this until you can place your hand on top of his head and he doesn't care.

You must understand that these are things that puppies instinctively do not like and that is why they resist. However, if a puppy doesn't like something, it doesn't mean that we should not do it. Just because a puppy resists something doesn't mean it's a bad thing. Earlier we talked about how babies often resist having their faces washed, or being strapped into their car seats. Does that

mean we should not do it? Again, the art of parenting involves teaching the puppy to yield to the authority and
learning that resistance is not necessary.

One of the best exercises that you can do is set your
puppy next to you as you sit and read or watch TV. At first
you will need to place your hand on your puppy to keep
him sitting quietly. If he tries to get up and leave, apply
pressure and say the word "stay." Do this for half an hour
or so. As you progress, your
puppy will sit there quietly without
your hand touching him. Believe
me; this exercise will be more difficult with some puppies than others. For example, it will be hard
for a puppy whose ancestors were
bred to chase and kill varmints to
sit quietly if he sees or hears a
small furry creature in the living
room. You may have a tough time
keeping your puppy calm if the
doorbell rings.

Placing your hand on your puppy
to keep him calm while you are sitting quietly is a good way to teach
your puppy to be patient.

It is also a good idea to pick your puppy up and place
him on your left side for a few minutes, then pick him up
and place him on your right side for a few minutes. If he
resists being picked up, pick him up and hold him in your
arms and wrap him up until he calms down.

More Holding Exercises

Another exercise that helps form a resistance-free relationship is holding the puppy's neck in your cupped

hands. While you are facing the same direction as the puppy, place your hands around the puppy's neck forming a circle. It looks like a choke hold, but you are very careful to not choke him. Your hands encircle his neck very much like a collar would.

Now, passively hold the puppy's head and neck still. If he tries to escape the hold, just hang on until he stops trying to escape. Once he relaxes, move his head into different positions. Hold his head up, hold his head to one side and then to the other side, and hold his head down. Do

Placing your hands around a puppy's neck is no different than placing a collar and leash on him.

Encircling your puppy's neck using your hands to teach him to yield to pressure rather than resist pressure makes leash training much easier.

this until there is no resistance.

A word of caution: Some puppies are very smart and do their best to cheat you into believing they are willing to yield to your authority. For example, you may be holding your pup's head in your hand and he is totally "relaxed," and you are passively holding him and all at once he jerks his head free and takes off. You have been "faked out." Don't feel bad; it happens to the best of parents at least once or twice. Just take hold of the leash and bring him back to you. Remember, one of the most important things to teach your puppy is to come to you *no matter what*.

You must understand that when you place a collar and leash on your puppy, you are attempting to impose your will. You are asking your puppy to go where you want to go and not necessarily where he wants to go. The leash and collar are nothing more than extensions of your hands. If you do these exercises successfully prior to trying to leash train your puppy, leash training will be much easier. On the other hand, if you let go of your pup every time he tries to escape your hold, there will be no progress and instead just continued (and even escalating) resistance. There must be a firm insistence, otherwise there is no progress.

A discussion of canine anxiety would not be complete without a word or two about canine stress-related compulsive disorder, sometimes referred to as obsessive compulsive disorder (OCD). Dogs engage in repetitive behavior such as constant licking, barking, tail chasing, and running in circles. This condition occurs in a fair number of dogs. I believe it is another manifestation of anxiety, and dogs that learn to control their anxiety are less likely to suffer from the disorder. If we expose them to stress early in life and get them through the anxiety, there is at least a chance we can teach them to control their anxiety later on.

The exercises that I have described will cause your puppy a degree of anxiety. You will learn to recognize an anxious puppy when you feel one in your hands, and by the same token you will learn what a calm and non-anxious puppy feels like in your hands. You will learn that if you insist, the puppy is very capable of learning to control his anxiety with your help. You will learn that if you allow your puppy to escape the control or pressure, he will never be capable of exercising self-control during periods of stress.

Previous Experience and Genetics

✿ ✿

Everyone knows that previous experience has an affect on behavior. However, most people are not aware that genetic makeup determines how the experience affects the behavior. Puppies come into our clinic every day and they have an experience. We do everything we can to make certain the experience is not traumatic. However, at some time or another that puppy will be asked to do something he does not like—for example, receive a vaccination via a hypodermic needle. Some puppies are sensitive and react dramatically to anything that might cause discomfort or pain, while others couldn't care less.

If it is not a shot that riles him, it may be taking the puppy's temperature, opening his mouth, trimming his nails, looking into his ears or a number of other manipulations included in a physical examination. These things are hard to accomplish if the puppy is vigorously resisting. Consequently, veterinarians hold the puppy or have someone else hold him until he stops resisting. The technique is called passive restraint; i.e., the puppy is held firmly while resisting and the hold is relaxed when there is no resistance and relaxation is praised with gentle stroking and talking sweetly to the puppy.

Most puppies are readily habituated and conditioned using this method. However, others are still very resistant.

It is the genetic makeup of the puppy that determines how he will react to the physical restraint. Age has some affect, but will not be as great a determinant as the puppy's genes. As I have mentioned previously, the sooner puppies can be habituated the better. Habituation can be very traumatic if not done in a skillful manner. In fact, I have seen many puppies that have been unintentionally habituated to resist rather than to yield. For example, if a person attempts to apply ear medicine and the puppy fights or resists, the person may assume the puppy is in great pain so they stop. What has the puppy learned? Well, the simple lesson is: All I need to do to prevent having my ears handled is resist and cry. While there may be some discomfort associated with the application of the ear medicine, in most cases it is not physical pain that causes the puppy to resist; it is the control that he is resisting. If you do not believe this, hold a puppy's head still *without* attempting to medicate the ears, or hold the puppy's feet *without* trimming the nails.

I remember a patient named Bobby and his owner Jim. Bobby had an ear infection that required the application of medicine to the ear canal every day. I treated the ear and asked Jim to treat it daily and return in ten days. When Jim and Bobby returned in ten days, the ear was no better. I asked Jim if he had been treating the ear, and he said he did once or twice but Bobby did not like his ears messed with and would not let him treat them. As I was treating Bobby's ears without him resisting, I asked Jim why Bobby would allow me to treat his ears and not him. Jim's reply: "He knows your are a doctor and are trying to help him." I said, "Right, do you think it was the sign or the white coat?" We both laughed and agreed that Bobby had the upper hand at his house.

I can speak from experience when it comes to resisting control. As a child I hated going to the dentist and I hated getting my hair cut, not to mention having my ears messed with. When I was growing up on the farm, I liked to swim in the local creek with the mud puppies and frogs and I developed an ear infection. I can remember resisting my parents as they treated my ears. I would scream and kick and really try to escape. However, I could not escape. They held me and calmed me, and when I calmed down I found that the treatment was not nearly as bad as I imagined. Like my granddad said, a fellow can get used to anything.

It is difficult for people to understand how a puppy can be so resistant and hysterical without automatically assuming that the pup must have had a previous experience that was traumatic or painful. I once examined a fourteen-week-old puppy that was resistant to having anything done to him. It did not matter what I attempted to do; he would have no part of it. The puppy was a basket case. It was the first time I had seen the puppy, and I turned to the owner and said, "I bet you believe this puppy has had a bad experience or has been abused."

She said, "All my friends are convinced he has been abused, but I have had him since he was seven weeks old and I know he has not been abused. I think his mother must have had a bad experience while he was in the womb."

I tried to assure the client that the puppy's behavior was not a result of his mother experiencing trauma during pregnancy. She was not convinced, so I explained that it really didn't make any difference what caused the puppy to be the way he was. It was not possible to undo what had been done. The important thing was to recognize the behavioral problem and try to fix it as soon as possible. The client said she wanted to keep the puppy and wanted to make him more enjoyable to live with.

Her reaction is very typical of those that are not aware of the influence genetics have on behavior. This puppy was very resistant to physical restraint because he was born that way and he had not been handled in a way that would teach him it was okay to be touched and held. Every time the owner would try to do something like take him for a walk on a leash or hold him when he didn't want to be held, he would resist frantically and she would yield to the resistance. The parent and friends could not understand how an otherwise sweet puppy could be so difficult.

As time went on, the puppy became more and more resistant because he had learned he could have his way any time he wanted. The longer a puppy such as this one goes without habituation and conditioning, the more difficult it is to accomplish a bond of mutual trust and respect.

I held the puppy for a few minutes, and every time he struggled to get away I held him firmly. After a while he did not struggle. He was learning to think about someone

other than himself. He would look at me as if to say, "What is going on here? Is there someone else in this world besides me?" As I worked with the puppy, he learned to trust me and would let me look into his mouth and trim his nails and do all sorts of things that he previously would have no part of. He even allowed me to lead him around on a leash. Each time I touched him and there was no resistance, I would pet and love him. Each time he resisted, I would hold him firmly until he relaxed, then I would praise him for relaxing.

The owner was astonished that her puppy could be so calm and tolerant in such a short time. In fact, the puppy was more interested and seemed more attached to me than his owner. He focused on me and would not leave my side. I told her he would do the same thing for her if she would work with him in a similar manner. She did, and when I saw the puppy two weeks later, he was a different dog and the owner was quick to tell me she had gone to her friends to show them how well he was doing.

Often, dogs are less assertive and resistant in a strange environment than in their familiar surroundings with familiar people. Many times the puppy has already established a relationship with the parent wherein he is the controlling member of the relationship. The puppy has not established a relationship with me, or if he has, he is not the controlling member and consequently he is not as resistant. However, if the puppy will become calm and relaxed in the clinic environment, there is no reason he cannot become thoughtful and trusting in his familiar surroundings with familiar people if the people have the time and the will.

Some dogs are by nature very suspicious or wary of different people and different environments. This natural wariness is a result of the genes the dog inherited from his forebears. Some dogs are wary of anything different. For example, I have seen dogs that were very distrustful of objects out of place in their familiar environment. If my friend Gus walks into our house and a piece of furniture has been moved, he knows it immediately. He looks around the room as though the thing or person that moved the object is still around.

Puppies and Autism

In her book *Thinking in Pictures*,[1] Dr. Temple Grandin, who is autistic, describes how she sees the world from an animal's point of view and explains how some people with autism are like fearful animals. She says they live in a constant state of fear, worrying about a change in routine or becoming upset if objects in their environment are moved. I would say she has a unique understanding of animals and has given me more insight into animal behavior than any other person.

Dr. Grandin also explains how some people with autism seek physical pressure to calm their anxiety. When

---

1   *Thinking in Pictures*, Temple Grandin, Vintage Books, 1996.

she was a young girl visiting her aunt's ranch, she observed how the cattle would calm down when the side panels of a squeeze chute applied pressure to them. When she saw how the squeeze chute relaxed the cattle, she crawled into it and asked her aunt to press the sides against her and to close the head restraint bars around her neck. She hoped it would calm her anxiety. Her description of what she felt follows:

"At first there were a few moments of sheer panic as I stiffened up and tried to pull away from the pressure, but I couldn't get away because my head was locked in. Five seconds later I felt a wave of relaxation, and about thirty minutes later I asked Aunt Ann to release me. For about an hour afterward I felt very calm and serene. My constant anxiety had diminished. This was the first time I ever felt really comfortable in my own skin."

After this experience, Dr. Grandin designed and built the first human "squeeze machine" that is used to relieve the anxiety of people with autism.

Dr. Grandin's work has helped me understand the importance of anxiety and its effect on dog behavior. I have seen dogs so sensitive that they vastly overreact when startled or frightened. For example, if a dog is walking down the street on a leash and a car backfires and frightens the dog, he may subsequently become frightened any time he is walking down the same street and comes to the point where the backfire occurred. I have known dogs that were in the front yard with their parent and were so frightened by a large truck rambling by that they would not want to go into the front yard again. I have also known dogs that have probably had a frightening experience in the back yard. However, the people in the household were not aware anything had happened and wondered why the dog refused to go into the back yard.

What frightens one dog will not necessarily frighten another. Some dogs react when going to the veterinarian, just as some children and even some adults react when going to the dentist. The experience may be the same for each individual, but the reaction is different.

In the course of my practice, I have had two patients that have had epileptic-like seizures (grand mal) upon entering the clinic. I had cared for the dogs since puppyhood and they did not start having these seizures until they were five and six years of age. The only time they had seizures was when they came to the clinic. One patient would have a seizure within twelve seconds after coming through the door. After two episodes, I suggested we treat the patient out in the parking lot and that worked. The second patient would have a seizure when the car pulled up in front of the clinic, so treating her in the parking lot was not an option. I went to the patient's home to treat her, and she did not have a seizure. Both patients were of the same pure breed.

Dogs that react so dramatically to their environment are very easily conditioned by one bad experience and are not so easily counter-conditioned. Although the following story is about cattle, it involves significant numbers and a controlled environment—the same for each animal.

Dogs and Cattle Are Very Similar When It Comes to Anxiety

The most dramatic example of how genetics can influence behavior was demonstrated a few years ago when we handled cattle at our family ranch. Each fall the cows and their calves are gathered. The calves are vaccinated and weighed then returned with their mothers to the pasture and revaccinated and weaned twenty-one days later. There were a hundred cows and calves in this particular pasture. The calves had been with their mothers since birth that spring. All of the cows were of similar genetic background; however, thirty of the cows were bred to a bull of a completely different breed. The remaining seventy cows were bred to bulls with a genetic background similar to their own. All of the cows and calves had been in the same pasture and experienced the same environment.

When we would drive or ride through the pasture, all the cows and calves, regardless of genes, reacted similarly prior to being handled. They had a predictable flight zone, but it was not extreme. In other words they were all relatively gentle and docile.

The flight zone is how close an animal will allow a person to approach without moving away from the pressure. This distance will depend on many factors: whether the person is someone the animals are used to, whether the person is on foot or horseback or in a pick up, and of course whether the animal has had a previous experience.

When the cows and calves were gathered and the calves were weighed and vaccinated that fall, all hell broke loose. Each calf was weighed individually and randomly in a small scale or chute (without side panels that squeezed down). When each of the thirty calves sired by the bull of the different breed were weighed, they went berserk. They could not tolerate the confinement or restraint and flipped upside down and bawled wildly. On the other hand, when the calves that were sired by our regular bulls were placed in the chute, they did not react wildly at all.

I cannot overemphasize the fact that the environment was the same for all calves since birth, and I believe that is very important to understand. After all of the calves were placed back with their gentle mothers, the thirty calves that went berserk were never the same. Their flight zone had tripled and when anyone entered the pasture, they threw their heads up and moved far away, watching every move. The remaining calves were as gentle as always and stayed with their mothers. Their flight zone was the same as it was prior to the "bad" experience.

Recently I was asked by a human psychologist who specializes in aggressive behavior how I would go about making a Hereford bull as aggressive as a Spanish fighting bull. Hereford cattle are known to be a gentle and relatively nonassertive breed, and it is unusual to find an excessively aggressive bull. On the other hand, all Spanish fighting bulls are very aggressive. I told him I would breed the most aggressive Hereford bull to the most aggressive Hereford cow I could find and repeat this process for several generations. He was somewhat dismayed that I would answer the question as I did. Most people answer the question by saying they could make the Hereford bull aggressive by being mean to him or abusing him by teasing and tormenting. The key is the comparison made between the two breeds. Anyone that knows animals knows that it is very difficult to make certain individuals aggressive no matter how they are treated. On the other hand, some individuals are aggressive no matter how they are treated. Social experience is very important, but genes determine how the individual reacts to the experience.

Extreme Resistance

I have said it many times and I will say it again: You will never know anyone's true temperament or personality until you have had a confrontation or an encounter with them. Any time you attempt to impose your will upon your puppy and there is resistance, you are having a confrontation. If the puppy's reaction to your imposition is *extreme*, you know your parenting skills will be tested as you attempt to develop a relationship of mutual trust and respect. On the other hand, if your puppy can become habituated to accept your authority and does not resist, there is no confrontation. Consequently, the relationship is one of trust and respect.

Puppies that exhibit violent and aggressive resistance and will not accept your control are many times very difficult, if not impossible, for ordinary dog lovers to parent. They are extreme when it comes to resistance and sometimes it is impossible for anyone to salvage them as acceptable members of society. The thought that "there are no bad dogs, only bad people in this world" is totally incorrect. Our institutions are full of people that do not behave in a sociably acceptable manner and many more are on the streets. Likewise, it is naive to believe every dog that is born can become an acceptable member of society.

Predicting Outcome

It is difficult to predict how a puppy is going to "turn out." Not long ago, a client told me she took her aggressive two-year-old dog to a professional behaviorist. When the puppy was eight weeks old, I advised the client that her dog was very strong-willed. I demonstrated to her the magnitude of his aggressiveness and resistance to controlling touches and holding. I told the client her parenting skills would need top-notch tuning to make this dog an acceptable member of the family. Two years later, the behaviorist told the client I should have known all along that this animal would not make an acceptable puppy for her, and I should have told her to return the puppy to the breeder. Here, he said, was an enormously and probably abnormally aggressive puppy. I felt like an idiot.

On the other hand, I have apparently been a top candidate for idiocy for wholly different reasons. I have recommended that people take puppies back to the breeder because of the young dog's aggressive behavior—then I listen as breeders tell me I am an idiot.

I try very hard to help people get along with their dogs and a very high percentage do great. I wish there were ways to reliably know if a relationship is going to work. If we could do that, I don't suppose there would be so many divorces. It is very traumatic for a family to be forced to give up a two-, three- or four-year-old dog that they can't live with. However, I believe it is more than a bit naive to expect us to reliably predict how we can get along in our animal relationships when we have such a difficult time with our human ones.

Dog Breeding

V ery few people actually know the origin of all the different dog breeds. They did not come from Noah's ark. However, what is amazing is that a species has been selected to do so many things not to mention selected for so many different looks. I don't believe anyone would argue with the idea that dogs are the most diverse single species on earth.

Every so-called purebred domestic dog breed is the direct result of a practice called inbreeding. Many generations of faithfully mating closely related individuals is required before a breed can be established.

Once a pure breed is established and a mating occurs between two individuals of that breed, there is some guarantee that the offspring will have the same physical traits as the sire and dam. For example, if you breed a purebred collie to a purebred collie, the offspring should look like a purebred collie. However, physical appearance of an animal does not tell the whole story. When it comes to genetics, there are dominate genes and there are recessive genes. As dogs are inbred, the occurrence of recessive genes is increased. Unfortunately many of the recessive genes are undesirable and some are lethal. That is what gives inbreeding its bad name.

It is very sad to see dogs develop disease as a result of genetics. People get attached to a puppy in about five minutes but the problem may not show up for several months or years. It is very unfortunate, but totally unavoidable. When dogs are so closely related, it is just a matter of the roll of the dice as to whether or not an undesirable gene is going to be expressed. For the most part, genetic problems are unavoidable at this time. However, great strides are being made to identify bad genes and some breed organizations have successfully identified the worst genes in their breed and are working to eliminate them.

Bad genes can crop up at any time and it can happen in the best of families. Every breed has undesirable recessive genes in their heritage and no one knows when they will appear. It is a sad but true fact.

At the same time, inbreeding can accomplish some truly amazing feats. I know a breed of dog that is the most loving and least aggressive breed in the world. I don't think there has ever been a dog of this breed that has ever been aggressive. However, as a result of inbreeding, a larger than expected number of individuals in this breed has genetic heart problems and skeletal problems. Thus, the dogs don't live as long as we would like.

There is an old adage frequently repeated in the animal breeding world: If you are breeding animals that are closely related and you have success, you are said to be linebreeding; if you fail and have bad results, you are said to be inbreeding.

Actually, linebreeding is a practice that enables the breeder to maintain a high relationship to one or more outstanding individuals within the pedigree while *reducing* the risk of exposing undesirable recessive traits. This practice allows outstanding sires and dams to "stamp" their traits on their offspring. Those outstanding individuals that predictably pass on their outstanding traits are said to be "prepotent." Unfortunately, dominant genes may mask the recessive genes and they can be carried for several generations without expression. Eventually, recessive genes become paired and when that happens the undesirable trait shows up.

Today, linebreeding is repeatedly practiced, but actual inbreeding has become rare unless someone is attempting to establish a new breed. The genetic diseases we see today are, in part, a result of the inbreeding done many generations ago when the breed was established. If intensive inbreeding went on today like it did as the breed was being established, we would see many more problems than we do. It is truly amazing we don't see more problems when you analyze how closely related dogs really are.

One of my veterinary textbooks[1] lists 285 different genetic defects that occur in different dog breeds and

---

1   *Textbook of Veterinary Internal Medicine*, Stephen Ettinger and Edward Feldman, 5th edition, Saunders, W.R., 2000.

lists the breeds in which these defects are most likely to occur. There are forty defects listed for the eyes alone.

After I had been in practice a few years, I called one of my veterinary school professors to express my frustration that many of the problems I was seeing were a result of genetic disease and were incurable. After I cried on his shoulder about the dogs that I could not fix, his consoling words to me were: "George, remember they don't breed dogs for good health; they breed them to keep veterinarians in business."

While he was right that dogs are not bred for good health, the reality is that man's first attempts to develop breeds of dogs involved perpetuating behavioral traits that gave dogs utility—traits that would benefit man's desire to survive or help him do his work. Dogs were bred to help man hunt and retrieve his prey as well as gather, herd and guard his flocks. Dogs were bred to help man fight his wars and guard his palaces. Dogs were bred to kill varmints such as rats. Dogs were used as beasts of burden and to pull wagons and carts as well as sleds. One of the most highly specialized dogs I can think of are dogs bred to be bed warmers. Some king was said to have had ten or twelve to keep his bed warm. They are small dogs with very thin skin and a thin hair coat. You can't believe how effective they are until you have slept with two or three.

A dog that has been bred to warm a bed is very different from a dog that has been selected to hunt game or guard sheep. Among hunt dogs, there are many varieties. Scent hounds go after their prey with their noses to the ground following a scent trail. Sight hounds chase their prey by keeping it in their view. If they lose sight they may use their noses to some extent but once they see the prey again the chase is on.

Dogs that were bred to hunt and kill varmints are very efficient using both sight and scent. Quick movement catches their eye and they go after whatever moves. The combination of excellent sight, excellent scenting ability, and terrific tenacity make varmint dogs very efficient at ridding an area of small furry creatures. They also can be hard on the cat population if they are not taught to control their aggressive tendencies.

Herding dogs or stock dogs are also very complex. They have to be somewhat aggressive by nature to control and dominate animals larger and stronger than they are. Herding involves pressuring other animals to go where they don't necessarily want to go. To put a 1,200-pound cow where she doesn't want to go when you weigh only forty pounds requires a degree of assertiveness or dominance as well as determination. All dogs have a degree of herding instinct. It is just more pronounced in dogs bred for herding than say dogs bred for guarding.

Varieties of herding dogs are very different in the way they handle livestock. Some have a strong gathering and holding instinct while others have a strong urge to chase and bite. Some go for the head rather than the heels and some go for both head and heels. Some are more aggressive by nature than others. Some breeders produce dogs that are better for sheep because they are less aggressive or less apt to bite, while others breed strains that are more suited to herding cattle. I even know some breeders that breed stock dogs specifically for dairy cattle verses beef cattle. This is an example of how finely tuned some breeding programs can become.

There are several breeds that are known as sheep dogs but are in reality guard dogs.

These are larger and aggressive breeds that are put with the sheep at a young age so they will bond with them. The idea is to have the large dog believe he is a sheep, and if a large predator such as a wolf comes along to get a helpless sheep, the big dog will chase the wolf, coyote or other dogs away. If trained properly, these dogs serve the purpose well. However, if the dog does not bond with the sheep in a proper fashion, he can and often does become a sheep killer rather than a sheep protector.

We have dogs that specialize in pointing and retrieving game. It is fascinating to observe the difference between a retriever (scent hound) and a herding dog (sight hound) and how they go about retrieving a ball in the back yard. Throw the ball for the retriever and he will go to it by sight but if he loses sight of the ball he will hunt for it with his nose until he locates it. Throw the ball for the herding dog and he will go for it as long as he can see it. If he loses sight of the ball he continues to look for it with his eyes.

To test young bird dogs for pointing instinct, trainers tie a quail wing onto a fishing pole and a short string and flip the wing down. If the puppy has strong pointing

instincts he will point by sight and that is good. It demonstrates that the puppy has a strong inborn trait to point. However, if you do too much to stimulate sight pointing, it takes much longer to teach the puppy to rely on his nose to point the birds. You see, bird dogs are supposed to point when they smell the birds.

When we get to the toy breeds we get a little of everything. Toy breeds are dwarfs of larger dogs—true achondrodystrophic dwarfs that have been selected for physical appearance (small size). The genes that influence physical appearance were the criteria for selection and the genes that influence behavior came along for the ride. In the past twenty-five years, breeders have made great strides selecting for behavior within the toy breeds. It is unbelievable how closely related the Chihuahua breed is to the Great Dane breed.

Although dogs were originally bred for utilitarian purposes, that is not so true today. There are relatively few people that breed dogs for working purposes, with the exception of dogs bred for herding, pointing, retrieving, guarding and attacking. However, some dogs bred for specific work have become desirable for their beauty, and when you select for looks only and ignore the genes that effect behavior, all types of undesirable behaviors crop up and then several generations are required to fix the problem.

Selecting for behavior traits can be very intricate and challenging. I know a breeder of herding dogs that has gone to great lengths to not only select for outstanding herding instinct but also has worked hard on selecting for behavior that influences a dog's willingness to be controlled. For example, the stock dog must have the instinct to control the stock and at the same time must be willing to be controlled by the stockman, otherwise there is no control and the dog does it his way or not at all. That is exactly what happens in some cases. The dog has great instincts but will not work unless he can do it the way he wants to.

When we select for certain behavioral traits and intensify them by inbreeding, we change the equation. For example, if we intensify the genes that influence prey chasing and killing such as with varmint dogs, we create a dog that will dive into a horde of rats and kill as many as fifty without stopping. He will kill rats until there are none left. By selective breeding we have changed the dog from a predator to a rat killer.

The same thing has been done with fighting dogs. Certain breeds of dogs have been bred to fight other dogs for sport. The problem with such a practice is that the normal dog behavior is abolished and what I call pathological behavior becomes manifest. A pathologically aggressive dog can turn into a human killer if the right button or wrong button is pushed. If a small child is playing and falls and skins his knee and starts running and screaming, a trigger may be pulled and the dog goes into a frenzy. The dog loses all contact with reality and goes into the chasing/fighting/killing mode. It is very difficult, if not impossible, to teach some of these dogs to control their instincts and urges or self-control.

The most predictable thing about a dog breed is their appearance. We can usually tell what breed we are dealing with by the way they look. Behavior within a particular breed is not quite so predictable. If a breed has been developed to retrieve, most of the individuals within the breed can probably be trained to be reliable retrievers. However, other behavioral characteristics are not so reliable. For example, one individual may be an excellent retriever but is very aggressive and hard to live with.

Field trial retrievers are highly specialized dogs that go through intensive training to achieve the desired task of competing in very complex trials. These dogs must be very "tough." The training is so intense that a "soft" dog cannot stand up to the pressure. When you select for dogs that are intense and can take the rigors of a field trial career, you may be selecting for dogs that are not so easily trained by ordinary dog lovers and consequently may be too tough and too energetic.

Dog Shows

Dog beauty contests, known as dog shows, are a relatively recent phenomenon. For many years, the most important consideration given show dogs was their looks. Physical traits such as color of hair, length of hair, length of nose, color of eyes, shape of head, and type of hair were given great consideration. Structural features that had little to do with function became important. The list goes on and on.

Recently, more show breeders have started looking at behavior as an important consideration. Show dogs are not required to do much of anything except look pretty. However, when a large proportion of the individuals in a particular breed becomes hard to live with and resistant to learning appropriate behavior, you know something needs to be changed.

When asked almost thirty years ago to talk to a local kennel club, I told the president of the club that his members did not want to hear what I had to say. He asked what I wanted to talk about, and I told him I wanted to talk about how dog breeding relates to behavior. He asked me if I really believed breeding had *anything* to do with behavior. I told him breeding had *everything* to do with behavior. I was right; his members didn't want to hear what I had to say and he got another speaker.

Recently I was asked to talk to the same club. I told the president I would like to talk about behavior and dog breeding. He said the club members would like that very much. It was a fascinating evening and everyone in attendance was glad to discuss the topic. Everyone, including myself, agreed there is more of a problem with people parenting puppies than there is a problem with breeding. Certainly there are exceptional dogs that are antisocial and extremely resistant to learning acceptable behavior, but most breeders these days do not breed those individuals. Most breeders today understand that behavioral traits are passed from generation to generation.

What Breed?

One of the most frequent questions people ask a veterinarian is, "What breed of dog should I adopt?" My answer is, "What breed of dog to you want?" People usually have an idea of what they want based on some dog they have known that has impressed them. Unfortunately, if they've seen an outstanding dog of a particular breed, they assume it is the breed that made him outstanding when the individual dog may be outstanding because of superior parenting skills or a combination of genetics and parenting.

The reality is there is no particular breed that has a monopoly on goodness—when I speak of finding a puppy that is relatively easy to parent, I am simply referring to dogs that like people, are not overly aggressive, not overly submissive and not resistant to learning acceptable behavior. There is as much variation in behavior within a breed as there is between breeds. There are "bloodlines" or families of dogs within a breed that are fairly uniform when it comes to behavior. However, as a whole, there are many extremes within a breed. Some puppies within a breed are very difficult to parent and great skill is required. Some puppies are very easy to parent and grow up to be outstanding members of society regardless of parenting skills. A person that is fortunate enough to adopt an *easy* puppy does not understand how anyone can have a difficult time raising a puppy. But puppies are like children: You have to have more than one to learn how different from each other they can be.

It is ironic that people resist believing genetics have a great deal to do with behavior, yet they want a particular breed because they believe all dogs in that breed are alike. If there is a particular breed of dog you like and want to know how virtuous it is, go to the book store or a pet shop and find one of those little books written about the breed. I call them "breed books." They are written by people that have spent their entire life breeding that particular breed of dog and are considered expert. Since they have been so devoted to "their" breed, they feel obligated to write a book extolling the virtues of their breed. Of the twenty "breed books" I have read, I found that all twenty breeds are loyal and loving. I think someone should write a book about dogs of mixed ancestry because they too can be loyal and loving partners.

Preconceived Ideas

Early in my career, I developed definite thoughts concerning various breeds of dogs. These thoughts were based on previous social experiences. At one time, I had several show breeders as clients. I remember one client in particular that bred a large breed thought to be sweet and loving by most dog lovers. My client's dog's particular bloodline was very nonassertive and almost all of the puppies were relatively easy for people to effectively parent. I recommended this particular breed to many families. Then one day a new breeder came to town with a different bloodline and I got a rude awakening. This particular line was very aggressive and very difficult for people to parent.

When people would ask me about this particular breed, I would tell them if they were going to get a dog of this breed they need to get it from the breeder with the dogs that were not so aggressive. When the lady that bred the aggressive dogs called and wanted to know why I didn't recommend her dogs, I told her she would have to change her breeding program and I would need to see some evidence that ordinary dog lovers could live with her dogs.

The breeder knew she had a problem, but was hesitant to change her breeding program because her dogs had other outstanding characteristics and she was winning in the "show ring." I convinced her to be more selective concerning aggressive behavior, particularly fear aggression, and in a few generations she made great strides. It was rewarding to see the progress.

I am not suggesting that people select the most submissive dogs they can find and breed them. I am suggesting that people avoid selecting extremes when it comes to behavior or any other trait.

Some people believe you can breed a Bulldog to a Greyhound and get a dog that can run and fight at the same time. It doesn't work that way. Crossbreeding is the practice of mating two individuals from different breeds. A true crossbred dog would be from purebred parents, while a so-called mixed breed would be of parents of mixed heritage. When you cross and mix breeds, you do lessen the chances of genetic disease and increase what is known as vigor. However, you loose predictability concerning physical characteristics and, to some extent, behavior characteristics.

Over the years, I have been exposed to many different bloodlines within the same breed. I remember one breed that I thought to be very resistant to being touched and made generalizations about that breed. However, I later found those individuals within a particular bloodline of the same breed to be very non-resistant. That is why it is so difficult to make generalizations about a breed's behavior. I have found there are individuals from every breed that make excellent family members. I will say you have a better chance of finding a "good dog" in some breeds than others, but that may depend on what part of the country your dog comes from, or in other words, it may depend on the breeder.

Hormones and their Effect on Behavior

❋ ❋

How hormones effect behavior has been debated for a very long time. I can remember when the experts told us infants were sexually neutral at birth. I never did believe that theory; in fact I don't know of any livestock producers or veterinarians that did. Sex hormones have a profound effect on behavior, and I can tell some pretty good stories to illustrate my point. Still, the impact of hormones depends on the individual.

Thirty years ago, pet owners were not as interested in getting their pets spayed or neutered as they are today, and I had an opportunity to make several observations concerning the effects of removing the so-called sex glands of animals.

I particularly recall how some female cats would become very sensitive to being touched in certain areas and would become very irritable and at times aggressive. We said they had nasty dispositions. Such behavior is also associated with a condition known as cystic ovaries in female horses. Since these cats had not been spayed, I suggested that they might have cystic ovaries and they should be spayed (surgically remove the uterus and ovaries). When we operated on these cats, their ovaries indeed were cystic, and after they were removed, the cats' dispositions improved. However, that is not the end of the story. Some of these cats, after a few years, would revert to the same old behavior—nasty. Since they had already been spayed we couldn't do it again. If you are convinced hormones influence the unwanted behavior exhibited and you have removed the organ that produces the hormone, what do you do next? You look for an explanation for the behavior. Is the behavior a result of hormones being produced somewhere in the body other than the gonads (extra gonadal), or did the hormones that were produced prior to the surgery have a lasting effect on the brain? I suspect a little of both scenarios exist.

Please understand that all of this took place prior to the advent of animal psychoanalysts and psychogenic drugs. Consequently, we were very primitive in our approach. I had been told by one of my veterinary school professors that progesterone was "Mother Nature's tranquilizer." Consequently, when someone would come to me with a female cat that was acting nasty and I could find no reason other than a possible hormone imbalance, but the animal had already been neutered, I would suggest we try "Mother Nature's tranquilizer." As a result of carefully selecting the cases in which the hormone was used, I had several nasty cats under my care that had become sweet. In fact the owners of these cats referred to the hormone shot as "the sweetness shot."

At one point I had several patients that were owned by ladies that worked together in a nearby banking facility.

Occasionally when I would go to the bank, one of the ladies would mention it was time for her cat to get her "sweetness shot." One day one of the ladies brought her cat to get its sweetness shot. She told me that one of her fellow workers was being nasty, and how she told her she was going to have Dr. Gates give her a "sweetness shot" if she wasn't nice.

There is no question that progesterone effects behavior; in fact, this hormone has a profound effect on metabolism. I have seen intact female dogs that have what is known as false pregnancies, during which everything happens as though the animal is pregnant. Mammary glands develop and nesting occurs. The animal thinks she is pregnant but there are no puppies in the womb. They will even take inanimate objects to their nest and try to nurture them. Of course the object will not nurse, so many times the "mother" will nurse herself.

Also during a false pregnancy, the female dog may go weeks without eating and yet not lose one ounce of weight. Back when few female dogs were spayed, people would become very concerned that their dog would not eat even though she was healthy and not losing weight. Progesterone levels are high during these false pregnancies, and the animal's metabolism is at such a low level that they do not need to eat to maintain body function.

It is interesting to me that people in those days were more interested in spaying their dogs to prevent false pregnancies than to prevent actual pregnancies. They could not stand to see their dog not eat for weeks at a time—even though the owners would be told their unspayed female could develop a life-threatening condition known as pyometria (a uterus full of pus) and spaying prior to one year of age could virtually prevent breast cancer.

Males have their own special problems with hormones, including eating. Neutered animals have better appetites than intact animals, and neutered males are under less stress and not as concerned with procreating as they are with eating. I have seen large breed intact males lose 20 percent of their body weight during the heat of a neighboring female. The owner in most cases did not realize there was a female in heat in the neighborhood and would bring the male in to be seen because he wouldn't eat and was losing weight. These poor males would have swollen and tender prostate glands and could become pretty irritable.

It is amazing the lengths intact males will go to get to a female in heat. I have seen large breed male dogs break out basement windows and climb into the basement of a home and mate with the female, so they are at risk of injury as well.

It is very interesting to observe the difference in perspective that occurs with time. I was visiting with a younger colleague not long ago and explained one selling point we old-timers used to encourage owners to castrate their male dogs: it would help prevent prostate cancer. His response was that he sees relative few cases of prostate cancer and almost all the cases he has seen have been in castrated males. A person could get the impression that castration causes prostate cancer, but

his observation is influenced by the fact that almost all the male dogs he sees have been castrated. But earlier in my practice, we would see a higher incidence of prostate cancer because there were few males castrated.

Years ago, it was very difficult to convince people to "fix" their dogs, male or female. I will never forget one male dog that I cared for named Max. Max was very aggressive toward other males and was always getting into fights. Consequently, he would have to be brought in occasionally to be stitched up. He was very large, and I always wondered how the other dog came out during these fights. The lady of the household had the duty of bringing Max to get repaired, and she would always ask what could be done to prevent these episodes. I always recommended that Max be kept off the streets, but that did not seem to be an option so I would suggest that Max be castrated. That was not an option either because the lady's husband would object vigorously whenever she suggested that Max be castrated.

After several visits and many stitches, I suggested that we might try some female hormones to cool Max's jets. I told the Mrs. that I had used progesterone to modify the behavior of male and female cats and that it might work for Max. I mentioned that I had never used this hormone in a dog for this purpose and there was the possible side effect of breast cancer with prolonged use and the possibility of diabetes developing, but I thought under the circumstances that it was our best option. She asked, "What will I tell my husband?" I said, "Don't tell him."

We went ahead and gave Max a dose of progesterone and I didn't see him for at least six months. When Max came in for a routine checkup, he had gained weight and his coat was beautiful. I asked the Mrs. how he was doing, and she told me he was sleeping by the fireplace and act- ing like a different dog. I asked her what her husband thought about this change and she told me he said, "See, I told you Max would settle down." She never did tell him we were giving Max hormones.

A few weeks later she called on the phone to tell me Max was getting aggressive and wanting to run off again, and she was afraid he was going to get into more fights and wanted to know what to do now. I told her we could give Max a shot every six months. This went on for about three years and then, one day, the Mrs. brought Max in for routine vaccinations and during the visit wanted to make an ap- pointment to get Max castrated. I asked, "What will your husband say?" She said, "To hell with him! He took off with some young thing. We should have been giving him these shots!" We both laughed and scheduled Max for surgery.

For your information, progesterone is the hormone we use today to reduce the sex drive (libido) of men that repeatedly and aggressively attack women sexually.

Many dog owners are under the impression that cas- trating or spaying will cause a dog to "settle down." Surgi- cal removal of the sex hormone-producing organs does nothing to "settle down" a dog. Such operations may reduce some undesirable behavior such as leg hiking in males as well as male interdog aggression, and will prevent false pregnancies in females. However, it will not teach your puppy to think or cause him to be a thoughtful and considerate member of the family.

A father called me one day to ask if spaying his female dog "would help." I asked, "Help what?" "Help prevent her from biting my daughter," he replied. I said, "I don't think so," and I asked the circumstances of the bite. He told me the little girl was not bitten as bad this time as she was the time before. The previous bite required the daughter to have twenty stitches in her lip.

The dog was four years old and was very aggressive, and I asked if the father would consider putting the dog to sleep. The father told me he could not do such a thing, and when I asked why he said, "because we *love* her."

I do not tell such stories to ridicule people that keep dogs that scar their children for life. I tell them to point out just how deeply attached people become to their animal friends and why it is so important to teach puppies to be trusting and respectful and to exercise self-control in order to prevent such happenings.

A Few Thoughts about House Training and Using a Crate

❈ ❈

House training a puppy provides a great model for teaching a puppy self-control. If your puppy learns to control when and where he eliminates, you have made progress and there is hope you can teach him anything you want.

Not many puppy parents want their puppy to go to the bathroom in their house. They may allow them to bark incessantly, chase joggers, be aggressive, chew up the sofa cushions and jump and climb all over them, but they really get upset when they poop or pee in the house. The exception would be someone with a small dog that lives in an apartment and wants to teach his or her puppy to go to the bathroom in a litter box.

Puppies do not know you don't want them to go to the bathroom in your house, so you must impose your will and ask them to go where you want them to go. It is not much different than teaching your puppy some other behavior. It is a form of control and self-control. The greatest difference is that the puppy's instinct to go to the bathroom in the house may not be as strong as his instinct to bark at strangers, chase anything that moves, or be aggressive when someone gets too close to his food dish or favorite toy.

In my opinion, house training a puppy is one of the easiest things in the world to do. Even though I think it is easy, a lot of people still have problems doing it. In reality I believe the easiest thing to teach a puppy is to sit for a treat. Why do I believe this? Because every puppy in the world has been taught to sit for a treat, and I know a lot of puppies that are not house trained.

If you want your puppy to go to the bathroom outdoors, never let him go to the bathroom indoors. How simple is that? The greatest problem with house training is that it requires your time and your attention because puppies always wait until you are not watching to go potty in the house.

If you never allow your puppy to go potty in the house, he learns that pottying inside is unwanted behavior. Consequently, he gets into the habit of making the correct choice. Every time your puppy has an accident in the house it is several steps backward.

Some ideas that might help you are:
1. Keep your puppy on a leash and never let him out of your sight. If you can't watch him, put him in the crate. (I will discuss the use of crates and house training in greater detail later in this chapter.)
2. If your puppy goes to the bathroom in the house, you are not watching him closely enough.

3. If you catch your puppy in the act of going to the bathroom in the house, quietly tell him no and pick him up and take him outside. You interrupt his thought and he may not finish his job outside this time but he will not finish his job in the house either and that is a good thing.

Take your puppy out on a leash every two to three hours, to the same spot every time, and stand there for one or two minutes and ask him to go. Say something, anything, but say the same thing each time and you will teach him to go on demand in time. If and when he goes, tell him he is a good puppy. You can even give him a treat if you like. Be careful, however, because you may teach him that a treat is more important than going to the bathroom when and where you want.

   If he doesn't go to the bathroom in two minutes, bring him back into the house and watch him. Or if you can't watch him, put him in the crate. Most puppies will urinate every time you take them out— even if you take them out every thirty minutes. However, some puppies like to wait until they get back into familiar surroundings to have a BM. Most puppies these days have not been outdoors and the great outdoors is very exciting and distracting to them. A leaf blows and they are off, a car horn honks and they are distracted, a dog barks and they get excited, and they hate wet grass. Needless to say, it is going to take some time to get the puppy used to being outside. In the meantime, you must be patient and take your puppy in and out until he goes. If he attempts to go in the house, don't let him. If he goes outside, praise him lavishly.

One important aspect of house training is to never get mad. Remember, if your puppy goes to the bathroom in your house, it is your fault. You may get mad at yourself but don't take it out on the puppy. If your puppy has an accident, don't scold or reprimand in any way. He will associate the scolding with the mess and you but will not know where to go next time. The only thing he'll know for sure is to not go to the bathroom while you are watching, and when he does go he will deposit his waste where he thinks you can't find it. He will become sneaky. Remember, you may get your puppy house trained by scolding and/or rubbing his nose in it, but for every puppy that gets trained that way, I know of ten that don't.

Submissive Urination

This is as good a place as any to talk about a common condition know as "submissive urination." Submissive urination—urination when puppies get excited—is something they cannot control. If you can increase the puppy's confidence and self-control, he will be less apt to have the problem.

Submissive urination is a common condition that occurs when puppies become excited to see you or someone greets them new and different. It also occurs when puppies are scolded, feel threatened and when efforts are made to punish them. So *never* scold or threaten a puppy that urinates when he gets excited. If you do, the problem will become worse.

The best thing to do to prevent submissive urination is to ignore the puppy for the first few minutes when you come home. Have friends and neighbors restrain themselves when they visit. If you get excited or get mad, the condition will probably never go away. If you are calm and teach your puppy to calm himself, the condition can improve and often does.

Special Notes about Crate Training

Placing puppies in crates or cages is a very popular house-training tool these days. The crate or cage is supposed to serve as the puppy's nest or den, and puppies resist soiling their den most of the time. This method usually works quite well. In some instances, however, the crates cause a great deal of anxiety for both the puppy and the puppy parent. We must remember that in nature, puppies never sleep alone.

Coping with Puppy Anxiety

Anxiety is the major problem associated with crate training. When puppies are adopted and brought home to their new environment, they're usually quite anxious. Because most puppies have never spent a night alone in their entire life, isolation or solitary confinement is the worst thing that can happen.

Some puppies placed in confinement become frantic or hysterical. They can panic and cry for hours. People sometimes make loud noises in response to the puppy's crying, such as pounding on the crate, yelling, pounding on the wall or shaking cans full of coins. While these practices stop the puppy from crying and barking, they can also create more anxiety. The loud noise startles the puppy, and she feels threatened. When puppies feel threatened, they feel the need to escape. If they can't escape, they sometimes become aggressive. I've known people who make loud noises to quiet their puppy, then immediately reach into the crate to comfort her and find her cowering in the corner. If this person pressures the puppy by attempting to touch her, she might growl and bite the hand that feeds her.

Panic and crying for hours can cause puppies to become physically ill. Toy breeds that are susceptible to hypoglycemia, for example, can exhaust their sugar reserves during these panic attacks and vomit, have diarrhea, and sometimes go into convulsions. Large-breed puppies are not as susceptible to hypoglycemia but they may develop diarrhea and vomit from anxiety. These conditions occur because anxiety promotes the release of adrenaline, which makes the heart beat faster, makes breathing faster, and causes increased intestinal motility.

The Puppy's First Few Nights at Home

How can a puppy parent reduce the stress of isolation in a puppy that does not tolerate being alone? I see nothing wrong with sleeping with the puppy for the first few nights until he gets acclimated to his new surroundings and new family. Some people prefer sleeping on the floor with their new puppy, while others place the puppy in bed with them. The greatest danger of sleeping with the puppy in bed is the possibility that he may fall out of bed and injure himself or the puppy parent may roll onto the puppy. It is very common for people to sleep on the floor next to the puppy while he is in his crate and calm him during periods of anxiety. Or place the crate in the bed and calm the puppy when needed.

Some people are concerned that sleeping with a puppy will "spoil" him. I have never known a dog mother that didn't sleep with her babies. That's probably why we call them mothers. I don't believe that all puppies need to be slept with. However, I do believe it is less stressful for highly anxious puppies if someone sleeps with them and gradually gets them habituated to being isolated or confined to a crate. Putting ticking clocks and hot water bottles in the crate are popular calming techniques but they don't work for some puppies. Some puppies will calm themselves and not be stressed at all when placed in a crate, and that's fine too. Not all puppies require the same parenting skills.

Introducing the Crate at Bedtime

It's a good idea to introduce the puppy to the crate as soon as possible. If she cries, open the door, place your hands

on the puppy and apply firm downward pressure on the puppy to quiet her.

Once she's quiet, praise her with light touches but no pressure. You may have to calm the puppy several times with your hands. The key is to keep your hands on the puppy until she is completely calm. People tend to avoid touching puppies during so-called encounters or confrontations because they feel the puppy will become what is known as "hand shy." Just the opposite is true. If you use your hands to apply the pressure to calm the puppy and maintain the touching throughout the calming process, your puppy will learn to trust your hand as the calming force. If done properly the puppy will calm down the moment you move your hands toward her. Your puppy will learn to come to your hand.

Placing your hands on your puppy and applying pressure as you say *no* is a good way to teach him to calm himself while confined to a crate. Much time and patience is required with some puppies.

The puppy knows instinctively to cry for attention (positive attention), which is something natural that does not have to be taught. If a puppy gets too far from his mother, he will cry until his mother finds him or he finds her. Puppies do not cry for negative attention. That is a people thing.

If you can teach a puppy to calm himself while you are touching him, there's a good chance he can learn to calm himself when you are not there. The key to success when calming the puppy is to place firm pressure on him and say the word "no" when he is crying. The firm hold and pressure is an immediate negative consequence, and immediate negative consequences reduce the chance that a behavior will be repeated. The immediate positive consequence is no pressure when the puppy is calm. Immediate positive consequences increase the chances that a behavior will be repeated.

Some puppies do not know their parents don't want to get up every two or three hours. How would they know? If dogs are doing something you don't want them to do, you have to let them know! There's only one catch—you have to be there to tell them while they are doing it or better yet, let them know just before they do it. Timing is everything. You need to anticipate your dog's behavior because I can assure you that he is smart enough to antic-ipate your behavior. And, of course, you have to know how to communicate with him. We had a communication prob-lem at our house once.

Our Family Dog, Angel

I know first-hand about people getting up in the middle of the night to let the dog out. One night as my wife Pam and I were getting ready for bed, she slumped on the edge of the bed and exclaimed, "George, I am exhausted!" Our three sons were small, and I assumed she was exhausted because of the children, so I said, "Gee Honey, I thought I was helping with the boys."

"It's not the boys," Pam said. "Its Angel! She gets me up at 3:00 every morning. I wouldn't mind if she had to go the bathroom but she just putters around in the yard and eats grass." Angel was our twelve-year-old poodle.

"I had no idea Angel was getting you up every morning," I said. "The next time she wakes you up at 3:00, wake me up and I'll take care of it." Sure enough, when 3:00 AM rolled around, Pam shook my arm and said, "Angel wants to go out." I raised up and said, "Angel, get back to bed!" Angel didn't wake up Pam again at three in the morning for at least six months.

Angel had no idea that Pam would rather sleep than get out of bed at three in the morning. As I've said before, dogs are very presumptuous. They presume that if it's okay with them, it must be okay with you. Angel didn't come to my side of the bed to awaken me because she knew I would tell her to go back to bed. However, as long as Pam was willing to get out of bed, she imposed her will.

A typical puppy sleeps for about two or three hours and then wakes up. If she becomes anxious as a result of her isolation, she'll cry. If she is content, she may go back to sleep immediately or she may cry for a few minutes and go back to sleep. Or, she may cry and cry and, if not attended to, will have a bowel movement, urinate in the crate, or both.

You must understand that, in most cases, the puppy is not crying because she has to go to the bathroom. She is crying because she does not like to sleep alone and is experiencing anxiety. Evacuating her bowels or bladder is the result of anxiety. The dog is not punishing his new parents for something they have done or haven't done. When puppies are content, they can go several hours without going to the bathroom. I have seen many eight- to nine-week-old puppies sleep from 10:00 PM until 6:00 AM and not urinate or defecate.

The Sleep-Deprived Client

I have had several clients over the years that have suffered sleep deprivation due to their anxious puppy. I remember one who, when the puppy woke up every two hours, would get up and take the puppy out to go to the bathroom. Yes, he would urinate every time she took him out. She "knew" he had to go to the bathroom because if she didn't get up, he urinated in the crate.

Actually, the puppy went to the bathroom in the crate because of anxiety, and the puppy parent was suffering a little anxiety herself when she called and asked what she could do. I told her to come to the clinic and I would show her how to teach her puppy to calm himself. (Often people believe their puppy has a bladder infection. Sometimes they do, but most of the time they don't.)

The puppy, which was almost five months old by this time, was very anxious about everything. When I held him, he resisted rather strenuously. After a few minutes, however, he calmed himself. The parent placed her hands on the puppy at the same time I did and spoke to him when he was calm. After the owner worked with the puppy for a few nights by calming him rather than taking him out and telling him everything was okay, they both slept through the night and lived happily ever after.

It is fine to tell the puppy everything is okay once they have calmed themselves; however, it is counterproductive to tell the puppy everything is okay during periods of anxiety or excitement. When you pet and praise your puppy during these behaviors you are increasing the chances he will repeat the anxious behavior as a result of the immediate positive consequence.

If people are having problems at night, I ask them where they place the crate. Often, they have placed the crate as far away from their bedroom as possible. Sometimes that works and sometimes it doesn't. If it isn't working, I ask the parent to place the crate in their bedroom and work on teaching the puppy to calm himself. This usually works quite well, and the puppy and parent form a stronger bond.

Some people worry about establishing such a strong attachment; they worry that the puppy will suffer separation anxiety as an adult. Puppies that are taught to calm themselves (to develop self-control) are less likely to experience any type of anxiety and, as a result, are much more likely to be stable emotionally when they grow up. (It is not unusual for adult dogs three to five years of age to experience anxiety. However, if they have been taught to control their anxiety as a puppy, it is much easier to help them as adults.)

Daytime Problems

If there are no problems during the night, I ask my next question: "How are you getting along during the day?" Often people have their puppies in the crate at bedtime and get along just fine. The puppy sleeps all night in the crate and has no anxiety attacks. If they put the puppy in the crate during daylight or waking hours, however, the puppy has a panic attack, crying wildly as though in severe pain. On those occasions when the parent must place the puppy in the crate and leave the house for only an hour or two, they find the crate—and the puppy— covered in feces.

The puppy soils the crate because she has not learned to accept the control of the crate during the day. I had calls from three different clients in one day asking why their puppy could sleep all night without having an accident in the crate, but if they left the house for just an hour or two, their puppy would have an accident in the crate. One lady had left the room for only twenty minutes when she came back to find her puppy covered in feces.

This problem is usually a result of placing the puppy in the crate during the day and letting her out when she cries. It's much easier for a puppy to accept confinement at night, when the lights are out and everything is quiet. During the daylight hours, there's a lot more activity. The puppy knows it and doesn't want to miss anything!

To fix this problem, I ask the parent to place the puppy in the crate during the day while they are in the house. If the puppy gets anxious and cries, I tell them to open the crate door and place their hands on the puppy and apply a quieting pressure. If the parents teach the puppy to be calm while they are in the house, there's a good chance the puppy can calm herself while they're gone.

Whether or not a puppy needs help learning calming skills depends on the puppy. Some puppies are anxious for a few minutes, then relax. Others become hysterical and stay that way for hours. Those that become hysterical obviously need help.

First Signs of Separation Anxiety

Some puppies do great in the crate all night for several months, then all at once start defecating or urinating in the crate. Usually this happens with a puppy that has been in a crate at night from puppyhood, and the crate is located as far from people as possible and the puppy has not learned self-calming skills.

As the puppy matures socially, he becomes more and more attached to the people in the household. When he awakens in the night and is away from the family, he becomes anxious. This is a common type of separation anxiety. Why wasn't he anxious three to four months ago? Because he was not yet so attached, and anxiety increases with age.

Many times, the anxiety is so pronounced that the puppy will have loose stools or diarrhea. The best way to cure this problem is to put the puppy and the crate in the bedroom with the parent or parents and calm the puppy in the cage when he becomes anxious during the night or early morning.

Additional Notes about Crates

Some puppies are very resistant to going into the crate. Feeding them in the crate helps. Make the crate as pleasing a place as possible. Leave the door open and let the puppy go in and out of the crate. Remember, if you take your puppy out of the crate while he is crying, you are applying a positive consequence for unwanted behavior and you are increasing the chances that he will cry louder next time. Calming the puppy requires a firm insistence; otherwise there is no progress, just continued resistance.

I know people who believe putting their puppy in the crate when he misbehaves will teach him something. They believe "time out" will teach a puppy how to be thoughtful and considerate and there is nothing I can say that will convince them otherwise.

What Size Crate?

People like to buy crates that will work for the puppy when he is full grown. They don't want to buy a new crate every few months. That is fine, but a large crate for a small puppy doesn't work very well sometimes. The crate is too large and the puppy gets up, goes to the bathroom in one corner and goes back to bed. The puppy needs sufficient room to curl up and lay down, but any more room than that is an invitation to use the excess space as a bathroom. If you buy a large crate for a small puppy, use something to make it smaller. For small breeds, boxes work fine. Larger breed pups chew pasteboard boxes into small pieces. I have known people to use bricks to make the cage smaller. That is great if you don't want to move it.

House training a puppy should not be that difficult, but I have seen entire books devoted to the subject. As I said at the beginning of this chapter, house training is an excellent model for understanding how one teaches a dog to do a lot of different things. And it is a lot like other behaviors: If your puppy uses your house for a bathroom, don't ignore it because he may continue that the rest of his life. The sooner he learns what you want, the better. Crate training is a helpful tool, but do not believe it is an easy way out of a time-consuming job. If you spend as much time teaching your puppy trust, respect and self-control as you do house training him, you should have the best dog possible.

8

Respect or Intimidation

❀ ❀ ❀ ❀ ❀ ❀ ❀ ❀ ❀ ❀ ❀ ❀ ❀ ❀ ❀ ❀ ❀ ❀ ❀ ❀

I hear all the time that it is a good idea to simply ignore unwanted behavior and it will go away. If your puppy growls at you when you get too close to his food bowl, give him his space and stay away from his food bowl. If your puppy growls at you when you attempt to move him from your lap, leave him alone until he wants to leave. If your puppy growls at you when you attempt to take something from his mouth like a favorite toy or chew-strip, remove it permanently from his environment so that the situation will not reoccur. If your puppy is lying in the middle of the hallway or room, walk around him. If your puppy is chewing on your hands, give him a toy to chew on and keep your hands to yourself. And—one of my favorites—if your puppy is overactive or hyper, exercise him until he is tired.

All these strategies avoid conflict or a confrontation at all costs and they give cause to ask some serious questions: If you avoid going near your dog's food bowl for fear of getting bitten, are you showing respect or intimidation? On the other hand, if you go near a puppy's food bowl and he doesn't threaten you with aggressive behavior because he has received an immediate negative consequence in the past, is he intimidated? Or is he respectful?

Human Behavior that Causes Dogs to Become Anxious

There are many human behaviors that increase the chances of certain dogs becoming anxious and aggressive. One of the most common behaviors that causes a problem is scolding. I have people tell me all the time their puppy "sasses back." I say if you do not scold your puppy, he would not react in such a way. When people scold puppies, they usually are angry and they raise their voice and usually try to get into the puppy's face. They might even point their finger and make threatening gestures.

In my opinion, the puppy perceives this behavior as a threat, and when puppies feel threatened they usually do one of two things: They leave the scene or challenge the threat. Neither fight nor flight is a desirable behavior in a family member. It does nothing to establish a relationship of mutual trust and respect.

Instead of scolding your puppy if he is doing something wrong, call him to you, and if he comes, talk to him. Place your hands on him and apply pressure and say no. Then hold him next to you and gently praise him for being compliant. If he doesn't come to you when you say his name, you need to work on the mutual respect and trust aspect of your relationship. Go to him quietly and calmly and place your hands on him and apply downward pressure and say no, and then praise him—and then you and the puppy just go do something else.

Remember—the negative consequence for unwanted behavior must be immediate. The puppy must be in the act of whatever it is you don't want him to do. If he has already done something you don't like, forget it and try to do better next time. I suggest puppy parents keep a leash attached to the collar and keep the puppy close to them any time he is not confined to his crate. If you do not take the time to supervise your puppy, you cannot expect him to learn to think about what he does.

Another human behavior that causes problems is chasing after the puppy for whatever reason. The person usually starts off by yelling at the puppy and moving toward him at the same time. No self-respecting pup is going to tolerate such a threat and is going to take off. The person is not likely to catch the puppy unless he is cornered, and if the puppy has no escape there is not much left to do but fight.

If the puppy is kept on a leash, you can bring him to you and have your talk. You never call your dog to you and punish him because there is no need to ever punish your puppy. But you can call your dog to you to have a talk—a talk with your hands. The idea is to prevent bad habits before they happen.

When puppies are running at large, they can develop bad habits easily. One of the best places for a puppy to develop bad habits is the back yard. People that leave their puppy in the back yard unsupervised are asking for all kinds of problems and usually end up with a few, then tend to blame others for what they have created.

We dog lovers have come up with a multitude of different ways to stop unwanted behavior without laying a hand on the puppy. This is primarily a result of the puppy being older and more mature and thus posing a threat to the parent of getting bitten if they touch the puppy in a controlling manner. Some techniques that are commonly employed are cans full of rocks or coins. The parent shakes the can to make a loud noise to distract or startle the puppy. Squirting water or vinegar at the puppy when he is doing something wrong is another method. I have even known people to use air horns to startle the puppy. Lots of people use a rolled up newspaper or magazine and pound it against some object to frighten the puppy if it is doing something wrong. Would you do these things to your child? Although these techniques in many cases stop unwanted behavior, they do little to form a relationship of mutual trust and respect.

When someone mentions shaker cans and squirt bottles, I always think of the anxious young lady that came to my office one Saturday morning crying her eyes out and telling me she was going to have to find a home for her ten-month-old puppy that she dearly loved. It seems that Brandy was a fun-loving puppy and liked to play a lot. He had grown to seventy-five pounds and did pretty much as he pleased. Mindy had taken Brandy to obedience classes, and he was a good student in class. However, at home he was out of control. Mindy had been told she needed to really "wear Brandy out" so that he would be easier to control. So, Mindy faithfully went out each morning and threw the ball for Brandy to fetch. Brandy liked the game so much, he would not stop playing.

If Mindy tried to take the ball and go into the house, Brandy would block her way. He would insist rather firmly that they should continue the game. Mindy was late for work several mornings because of Brandy's insistence and went to a professional for help. The pro told her to shake a can full of coins to stop the behavior. Brandy promptly grabbed the can and ran off with it and continued to block the entrance to the house and even went so far as to grab Mindy's clothes and pull her away from the house. At one point, he grabbed her by the arm as she attempted to go into the house. The next thing she was told to do was squirt Brandy with water from a squirt bottle. That really made Brandy mad and he became aggressive and growled and snarled at Mindy and the bottle. That is when Mindy came to my office in tears.

Brandy was an active, out-of-control puppy that had no idea what Mindy wanted him to do. He didn't know he was making Mindy late for work because of his insistence. Once Brandy learned to think about someone other than himself, he was a great dog. He was very willing to be controlled by my hands. He resisted at first, certainly, but it did not take long for him to learn to yield to the pressure and exercise self-control. I showed Mindy many of the techniques contained in this book, with the result that the dog became a great companion. Six years later, Mindy and Brandy still get along well. Consequently, she is no longer intimidated.

When the subject of intimidation and respect comes up, I always think of a dog named Millie. Millie was from champion bloodlines, and the family was very proud of their newfound friend. Millie grew to sixty pounds by the time she was one year old and she was determined to be top dog. By the time she was two, she had bitten every member of the family except the father. When anything was said to the father about Millie's behavior, he would say there is nothing wrong with her and that the rest of the family just didn't know how to handle Millie. They told him the only time Millie bites is when someone does something she does not like, and he never did anything Millie didn't like. Until *one day*.

She had bitten the daughter because she got too close to Millie's favorite toy and she had bitten the son because he got too close to Millie's food bowl. Millie bit the mother as she was wiping off Millie's feet. The solution to this problem was to give Millie her space and avoid conflict. So they took Millie's favorite toys away and stayed away from her as she was eating. Needless to say, the mother did not wipe Millie's feet any more.

You must understand these bites were not ferocious or severe; just enough aggression to get what she wanted. Everything went fine until one day when, as the father was washing his brand new car in the driveway, Millie jumped into the front seat with muddy feet. The father became very mad and yelled at Millie, which frightened her very much, but she would not get out of the car. He went inside the house and got some treats in an effort to entice her

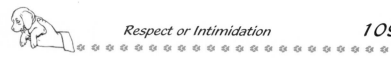

out of the car. No such luck. She was two years old and no one had ever challenged her authority like this before. Millie was having a major anxiety attack and the father did not realize it. If he had, he would never have done what he did next. He reached into the car and grabbed Millie by the collar and pulled. Big mistake! Millie attacked the father's arm very aggressively and stayed in the car.

This story has a sad ending. I cannot say with certainty that touching and holding Millie with purpose would have prevented her out-of-control anxiety and aggression. One thing for sure is that Millie did not learn to control her aggression on her own, and due to her size and the difficulty in reversing roles, coupled with the fact that the family did not want to live with an aggressive dog, Millie was put to sleep.

Some people get the idea that you can stare a puppy down and rein in their out-of-control behavior. I had a client in one day with a twelve-week-old puppy that was chewing on her pants cuff. As the puppy jumped and attacked the lady's leg, she stared at him very sternly. At one point she moved her face toward the puppy's face and he jumped at her and growled and snapped. She jumped back in shock and asked, "What am I going to do with this out-of-control puppy?"

This was another attempt to control a puppy without touching him. All that was needed was to hold the puppy until he accepted control and then he learned to exercise self-control.

Making Eye Contact with Dogs

One of the most important things to know about dogs is how their behavior can change in response to direct eye contact—staring at them. Because it is also one of the most poorly understood behaviors, relatively few people understand the consequences of having direct eye contact with some dogs. Unfortunately, it also explains why so many people are bitten in the face, particularly children. It is a small miracle that more children are not hurt and disfigured when the parents allow them to approach unfamiliar dogs.

You can analyze a dog's attitude pretty quickly by making eye contact. Apparently some dogs feel threatened by direct eye contact. While I can't be absolutely certain of what the dog is thinking, I can be pretty certain as to what might happen if you are not real careful. Eye contact triggers a sometimes uncontrollable instinct to lash out and bite. This characteristic is more pronounced in some dogs than others. In fact not all dogs have such a characteristic.

If you have direct eye contact with a dog that you are not totally familiar with, do it from a safe distance. If his mouth closes, his neck becomes rigid, and his pupils dilate, you can be in grave danger if you close the space between you and the dog. Never walk directly toward and keep closing the space with a dog that you have not bonded with. Although you may not be looking into the dog's eyes, he is in all probability looking into your eyes, and if you continue to close the space until you are virtually on top of him, he may attack your face.

In my opinion, it is never a good idea to initiate contact with a strange dog. If you approach a strange dog and don't have eye contact, you really have a hard time knowing what he might do, and if you touch him you could get bitten.

I remember when Old English Sheep Dogs were very popular with their shaggy faces. I still take care of a few, but nothing like in the late '70s and early '80s. I am always careful if their faces are covered with hair and their eyes are hidden from view because it is very difficult to know what a dog is thinking if you can't see his eyes. If I can't see his eyes, I look for the stiff or rigid neck and closed mouth.

In most cases, people who are bitten in the face by a dog are unaware of what they did to elicit such an aggressive attack. They approach the dog not thinking about eye contact. As they advance, the dog's eyes are fixed on theirs, but they aren't aware of this. As they get closer to the dog, the dog strikes (see illustrations on next page).

To understand how this mechanism works, you need only to watch herding dogs control livestock. The herding dog maintains eye contact with the stock. This is called "the eye" when the dog's eyes are fixed on the animal to be herded. If the animal being herded has eye contact with the dog or if they face each other, both animals usually stop and stare at one another. Many times the stock will yield to the dog and move away. However, if the sheep or cow being herded moves directly toward the dog when they are face to face, the dog grabs the cow or sheep by the nose. Some dogs just nip the herded animal and some will latch onto the nose or lip of the animal and hang on until shaken off.

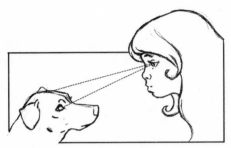

A person approaches a dog and may be looking at the top of the dog's head, where she intends to pet him. Meanwhile, the dog may have his eyes fixed on the person's eyes and the person may not be aware.

As the person gets closer, the dog becomes anxious and feels threatened. The person is still intent on petting the dog on top of the head.

If the person gets too close, an aggressive trigger is pulled and the dog strikes. Understanding how this mechanism works can save many people from being bitten in the face.

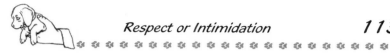

It is hard for people to understand why a family dog suddenly attacks a family member. However, in many instances, dogs have bitten family members in the face as a result of eye contact. I know of a case where a twelve-year-old girl was watching TV with her family. She was lying on the floor with her head on her dog's chest, using it as a pillow. She had done this regularly since the dog was a puppy. The TV program was very violent and scary. At one point, a loud scream came from the TV. The little girl lifted her head from the dog's chest at the same time that the dog lifted his head. They came eye to eye. The dog attacked the little girl in the face.

I am not suggesting the TV program caused the dog to become aggressive. There is a possibility, however, that the program caused anxiety or fear in the little girl and she released pheromones that aroused the dog's aggressive instincts. It is also possible that the loud high-pitched scream aroused the dog's aggressive instincts. Regardless, when they came eye to eye, he did not or could not control his instincts.

Since it is necessary for me to approach unfamiliar dogs every day, I will tell you how I go about introducing myself. Please understand that at least ninety-nine percent of the dogs we attend to are trusting patients and are not aggressive in any way. However, it is necessary to be somewhat cautious when doctoring unfamiliar dogs. The first thing I do is make eye contact. The eye contact is made from a safe distance. If the eyes dilate, the neck becomes stiff and the mouth goes shut, I immediately stop any forward movement and back away. If the dog has a soft and kind look (eyes not dilated, mouth open), I take a step closer. If eye contact doesn't bother him, I lift a hand. If he raises his head and follows my hand, I watch his eyes to see if his pupils are dilating and watch his mouth and neck. If his eyes dilate and his mouth closes, I take my hand away and back off. Next, in either case, I drop to one knee and call the dog to me with a hand full of treats. Dogs that are terribly anxious are not usually interested in treats. So if he eats the treats, that is usually a good sign. *But not always!*

If I call the dog to me and he doesn't come, I ask the owner (parent) to hand me the leash. I try to never initiate contact with a strange dog by actually touching it at first.

Anxious dogs are usually in the corner of the exam room when I enter the room, and it is not a good idea to initiate contact with a cornered dog. Anxious dogs prefer to escape the perceived danger, and if they cannot escape they become aggressive if pressured (fight or flight). After I have the leash in my hand, I again call the dog and if he doesn't come to me, I apply pressure to the leash, which applies pressure to the collar and in turn applies pressure to the back of the neck. (I prefer a plain and simple nylon or leather collar rather than pinch or choke chains.)

As the collar applies pressure against the back of the dog's neck, I get a real good idea of how he might respond to physical pressure. I am down on my knees and I pull so that the pressure is applied to the back of the neck.

You might ask why the big deal about pressure being applied to the back of the neck. When pressure is applied to the back of a dog's neck or to the top of his head, he perceives the pressure as an effort to control him. If he is not accustomed to being controlled, he will resist by elevating his stiffened neck and pulling back, or he may lash out uncontrollably and attack—hopefully just the leash.

I pull the dog toward me. If he resists, I pull him one step, then release, pull and release until he is next to me. While he is next to me and we both are facing the same direction, I stand up. If my standing over him doesn't bother him and pulling on the leash doesn't bother him, I will reach my hand down and touch him on top of the shoulders and move my hand up and down his back. While I do this, I keep my feet firmly planted and show no anxiety. After I have touched him up and down his back, I move my hand to the back of his neck and top of his head. I do this as I am standing over the dog and holding the leash so his head is pointed away from my body. Once he has allowed me to touch him all over, including the back of his neck and top of his head, I feel pretty comfortable and can begin my exam.

My methods for getting to know a dog are based on the way dogs naturally interact with each other and how they understand who is in control and who is not. Just watch the way two dogs interact and you'll see my point. They place a foot on top of the dog they are interacting with, or they may place their head on top of the other dog's neck. The dog that is receiving the pressure will

react in one of many ways. He may simply escape the pressure by ducking out, he may elevate himself and attempt to get on top of the dog that is applying the pressure, or he might growl and become aggressive toward the dog applying the pressure. Such aggression is usually inhibited and controlled. I would call all of the preceding reactions normal, depending on what social status the dog receiving the pressure believes he might possess. Another reaction is an uncontrolled attack on the dog or person applying the pressure.

My dog Gus and I learned this lesson the hard way. I learned my lesson in the examination room when I failed to follow my own advice while handling a Golden Retriever. Gus learned his lesson at the roping arena from a Labrador Retriever who was without question the top dog in her arena.

A client brought a four-year-old Golden Retriever in for an examination for skin problems. Since I had not seen this client or her dog previously, I introduced myself to the lady and turned to Sam and said hi. He looked at me rather sternly but not in a particularly foreboding manner. I offered him some treats and he reluctantly took them from my hand. I gave him a few more treats and petted him on top of the head lightly. Key word: *lightly*. Sam's eyes did not dilate when we had eye contact. However, I felt that his neck was a little stiff so in an effort to determine how he would react to pressure, I placed a little pressure on top of his head with my hand, which was a big mistake. Because as I placed my hand on his head, I had eye contact and at the same time moved my head and in a flash his eyes dilated and his mouth went closed. The next thing I knew he had my hand in his mouth and had his canine teeth buried to the bones in the palm of my hand. As I was standing there with my hand in Sam's mouth the lady exclaimed, "He is a Golden Retriever; they don't bite!" I said, "This one does and as soon as he opens his mouth I am going to take my hand out." After what seemed an eternity, Sam opened his mouth and I removed my bleeding hand.

The client was very concerned that Sam had bitten me and said she couldn't understand why he did such a thing. Sam had been through obedience training and would perform quite well on a leash. He would heel and sit and all the usual things dogs do that have been through obedience class. He would also sit for treats. I explained that when I applied pressure to the top of Sam's head and at the same time had eye contact, he perceived the gesture as an effort to control him and since he had never had anyone physically control him, he could see no reason to start now. The client cried out, "Oh my God, now I understand." I said, "understand what?" She went on to explain that when she gets down on the floor to play and wrestle with Sam and she puts her head on top of his head he growls at her. She thought it was just a game. I explained that it was a game to Sam but it could be a very dangerous game.

Gus's experience was very similar. When I go roping, I sometimes take Gus with me. The fellow that has the roping arena has two female labs that love people.

However, one of them is very intolerant of other dogs and can be very aggressive toward them if they overstep their boundaries.

Gus jumped out of the front seat of the truck and met Sally. Sally was on guard and was looking for any evidence that Gus might want to take over. Gus did not know Sally but he had interacted with many dogs in his two-and-a-half years. However, he had never met a dog like Sally. Gus did what he usually does; in what he thought was neutral territory, he initiated play. When dogs play, they try to get on top of each other, and when Gus put his paw on the back of Sally's neck and as they came eye to eye, she ripped into him with a ferociousness I had never seen in Sally. It was a vicious attack and one that Gus will never forget.

The next time I went roping and took Gus, he would not get out of the truck. After a while he decided to get out but he watched for Sally and when he saw her he looked away and if she approached he gave her plenty of space. Sally looked at Gus as if to say, "Don't try to take over and everything will be okay." Gus seemed to say, "It's your place, and I will stay out of your way."

The dogs in the two scenarios acted very similarly. In one scenario, a dog attacked another dog; in the other, a dog attacked a person. We think of our dogs as people, but they think of us as dogs. We think like people and they think like dogs. In both cases, the dog that attacked felt threatened. Sam was anxious because he was in an unfamiliar environment and a stranger was attempting to control him

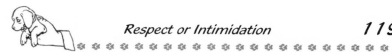

or possibly harm him. Consequently, he became aggressive although he did not control or inhibit his aggression as much as I would have liked.

Sally felt the same way about Gus. The big difference was that Sally was the top dog at her place and she felt Gus was threatening her position or attempting to control her or her territory. Consequently she became aggressive toward Gus, although she did not control her aggression as much as Gus would have liked.

Interestingly, the owner of Sam had no idea why Sam attacked my hand, and many times people do not understand why one dog attacks another dog. I have only one question: "Was Gus intimidated or was he respectful?"

Bringing a New Baby or Puppy Home to Your Dog

❀ ❀ ❀ ❀ ❀ ❀ ❀ ❀ ❀ ❀ ❀ ❀ ❀ ❀ ❀ ❀ ❀ ❀

I'm often asked how to introduce a new baby or puppy to the older dog in the family. The answer is simple: If you've taught your dog to be thoughtful and considerate of others and you have established yourself as the controlling member of the relationship, you won't have any problems. If you haven't taught your dog to be considerate, you may have a problem—a big problem.

It makes little difference whether you bring a new puppy or an infant into your home. In either case, your dog will become somewhat anxious. Anything new and different in the environment will cause a degree of anxiety. However, it is important to understand that anxiety is a part of living. The degree of anxiety depends on two different factors: just how anxious your dog is because of his genetic makeup, and to what degree you have taught your dog to control his anxiety.

The greatest concern of parents introducing a new puppy or infant is usually the safety of the individual being introduced. Puppies and infants are very physically vulnerable to adult dogs. In some cases, however, the people are more concerned about the existing dog than the individual being introduced.

The Most Common Problem

The most common problem occurs when a baby (toddler) or a new puppy either gets too close to the older dog's food dish or a prized possession, or disturbs the older dog's sleep.

Dogs that have not been taught to exercise self-control often attack the intruding puppy or toddler with uncontrolled aggression. It's a violent attack that can cause serious harm to the unsuspecting youngster. I have seen adult dogs kill puppies that ventured too close to the food bowl or prized possession. I have seen adult dogs disfigure small children for the same reason.

Aggression Sometimes Takes Time to Develop

Not all problems occur immediately after a new introduction is made. On occasion, problems don't occur until two or three years have passed.

One such situation occurred when a mother complained that her six-year-old dog had bitten her three-year-old daughter three times. The mother felt that her child was abusing the dog. Sadie had never bitten anyone prior to biting the little girl. Since Sadie was not aggressive prior to the arrival of the little girl, it must be the little girl's fault that Sadie was becoming aggressive.

Nothing could be further from the truth. I told the mother that she had allowed Sadie to grow to social maturity without teaching her to control her aggressive tendencies and, as a consequence, any time the child did something Sadie didn't like she would become aggressive. "You are saying I should have been getting after my dog instead of my child?" the mother asked. "Yes," I answered, "you should have started when Sadie was a puppy."

People sometimes have a difficult time understanding why their dog is at fault rather than their child. In this case, Sadie grew up doing everything she wanted to do. She was never asked to do anything she did not like because she resisted control. Her resistance was just enough to achieve the control she wanted. Just a hint of aggressive behavior was all that was needed to establish control. Consequently Sadie did not learn to exercise self-control. As Sadie matured, she became more and more intent on having her own way. She was picked up and held only when she said it was okay. She was touched only when she wanted to be. No one ever approached her while she was eating, and no one ever attempted to take something from her that she had in her possession. Sadie had grown up convinced she could do no wrong and, consequently, believed she was in control.

As the little girl became more mobile and was able to get close to Sadie's food and prized possessions, Sadie became more concerned about her top-dog status. When the child put her arm around Sadie to give her a hug, she was bitten rather severely. That was the first bite, and the mother thought it was her daughter's fault that Sadie bit her.

The second bite occurred when the child got too close to the food bowl as she was attempting to add food to the bowl. According to the mother, this bite was also the fault of the child because she was not supposed to feed Sadie. When Sadie bit the little girl in the face for no apparent reason, the mother thought there might be a problem with Sadie. There was a reason that Sadie bit the child: The little girl made eye contact and moved too close to Sadie's face. She invaded Sadie's space.

It is very common for children to get bitten in the face when they make eye contact with some dogs. These dogs do not bite children because they have been abused. They bite because they have not learned to control the aggressive mechanism that causes them to react.

A Self-Controlled Dog Is a Safer Dog

Small children are constantly being accused of abusing dogs. A small child can't begin to compete with a puppy when it comes to pestering dogs. I read recently that dogs should have a safe haven to escape pestering children. I saw no recommendation that the dog should have a safe haven from an exuberant puppy. If a puppy pounces on an adult dog's tail and bites and pulls on it, people think it is cute puppy behavior. On the other hand, if a child pulls an adult dog's tail, people can become very upset (with the child). If the dog bites the child, the child is accused of being abusive. I am not advocating that children pull on dogs' tails. I'm saying that it happens, and the dog should be tolerant enough to not attack the child.

A small child cannot do anything to a dog compared to what they do to each other. When dogs interact with one another, they are very physical. They chew on each other—on every place on their bodies including their ears. They paw at each other with their feet and poke each other in the eyes all the time. Watch puppies interact with adult dogs; they playfully attack an adult dog, jump on it, and chew on it; the puppy's pestering can be unrelenting. When this aggressive play is controlled, the puppies have a lot of fun and no one gets hurt.

It is difficult for me to imagine anything that a toddler could do that would justify an aggressive attack by a dog. By the same token, I can't think of anything a puppy could do to an adult dog that would justify an aggressive attack. Vicious attacks on the young and innocent are not tolerated in nature and they should not be tolerated in our society.

Habituating Brandy

An expectant mother once brought her one-year-old dog to our clinic for a routine exam and immunizations. The young dog behaved beautifully. He was the perfect patient in every respect. I couldn't help but comment on Brandy's behavior. I asked the mother to what she attributed Brandy's outstanding behavior. "I smothered him with love," she said. I asked her what, exactly, she meant.

She went on to explain that she and her husband were expecting their first child and wanted a dog that could handle being around a small child. With that in mind, she said she literally smothered him with love by touching him all over and actually laying on top of Brandy to get him used to being around a small toddler that was very likely to touch and pull on him.

Brandy had not been to obedience classes. If he had, I'm certain he would've been at the top of his class. His owner had not gone to a professional for help; she had used common sense and, in my opinion, had done a terrific job of habituating and conditioning her friend. She taught him trust, respect, and self-control. Brandy had learned to handle stress and pressure. Today, that first child is three years old. Everyone—parents, child, and dog—is doing fine.

Whenever I tell this story, people ask me what breed of dog Brandy was. It makes little difference what breed he was. He may have been an outstanding dog by virtue of his genes or he may have been an outstanding dog as a result of his environment. We'll never know for sure, but I suspect it was a little of both.

Trusting Your Instincts

People who are overly concerned about how a new pet or child in the household will affect the existing dog probably have good reason for their concern. They very likely see behavior displayed by the current dog that they recognize as a potential problem. Possibly, their own dog intimidates them on occasion; they own a dog that would bite the hand that feeds him. Possibly, they own a dog that does not handle stress well and becomes overly anxious. Consequently, they are anxious themselves about what might happen. Regardless of the reason, all dogs should be closely supervised when a new introduction occurs.

Equal Treatment?

People can become too concerned about which dog should be petted first or the most, and which dog should be fed first. Sometimes people even worry about whether or not the dogs get equal treatment. In my opinion, such thinking is another example of how people think—not how dogs think. If people would spend more time teaching trust, respect, and self-control to their puppies, they wouldn't need to concern themselves with such things as which dog eats first or gets petted first.

Eating Time at the Gates' House

Eating time is very interesting at our house. Gus and Gabby are fed in the kitchen, usually by my wife Pam. If one dog finishes before the other, he or she will stand and look at the other one as he or she eats. If I walk into the room, the dog that has finished eating will walk over to the one that is still eating, and the dog that is still eating will move over and share without looking up. Gus and Gabby were taught as puppies to share their food. I share my food; there's no reason why they can't do the same.

I recommend that a new puppy be supervised at all times, regardless of whether another dog is present. If the puppy cannot be supervised, place him in a crate or in an area where he cannot hurt himself or damage property.

The new puppy should be isolated from the first dog whenever there is no one present to supervise them. Otherwise, they should be together.

When introducing two adult dogs, keep them separated when they cannot be supervised. I recommend continuing this policy for at least two to three months, depending on the age of the dogs involved. If the adult dog is socially mature (three to four years old) and has been the top dog, be prepared for some aggression if the newcomer also thinks she should be the top dog. On the other hand, if you introduce two adult dogs that have learned self-control—they defer to humans and look to them as the authority—you will have very few problems.

It is not unusual for two dogs that have gotten along for two or three years to all at once try to kill each other. A typical scenario would be when a puppy is introduced to a two- or three-year-old dog. They get along fine as long as the puppy doesn't try to take over. When the puppy reaches an age that he thinks it is time for him to take over (usually two to three years) and refuses to yield to the older dog, there can be very serious consequences. I contend that if both dogs learn to accept the control of the parents, they will not fight if the parent asks them not to.

Extreme Behavior and Natural Selection

There is only one problem: Some dogs refuse to yield to anyone or any dog. I have seen mother dogs kill their own offspring if they refused to accept her control and resisted with violent aggressive behavior. There is no place for extreme behavior in nature, and those individuals that refuse to accept control do not have the opportunity to reproduce. Natural selection prevents extreme behavior from being perpetuated. However, when people enter the picture, natural selection is out the window. Unfortunately people adopt puppies that are extreme and feel as though they are failures when the dog turns out to be unfit as a family member. It doesn't happen a lot but it does happen, and I feel great empathy for these people.

Introducing Gus to Maddie Gates

One of the most interesting introductions was when Gus met Maddie, our Labrador Retriever. Maddie was five years old and a little bit anxious when we brought eight-week-old Gus into the house. Gus would jump at her and grab at her and she would just look away or leave the area. Pam was worried that Maddie would never be the same. Maddie was somewhat "depressed." After about a week, one of the boys came running to tell us that Maddie was playing with Gus and really having a big time. I went to the boy's bedroom to see the fun. When I entered the room, Maddie immediately stopped playing with Gus and came to my side. Jimmy said, "Daddy, Maddie doesn't know that you want her to play with Gus. Tell her it's okay." I began encouraging Maddie to play with Gus, and in six days they were playing together as though they were lifelong friends.

My wife and I have introduced several dogs and children to each other during the past thirty-four years, and no dog or child has ever harmed each other. We did have a

small poodle that became a little crotchety toward tod-
dlers in her old age, but if she didn't want to be bothered,
she would leave the room rather than bite. She found her
safe haven.

Closing Thoughts

❋ ❋

A s I have said throughout this book, the root cause for almost all dog behavior problems is anxiety. If you can teach your puppy to control his anxiety, you will have fewer problems. I believe the best way to teach a puppy to control his anxiety is to teach him to think rather than allow his instincts to rule his life and yours. I believe the best way to teach your puppy to think and to control his instincts is to hold and touch him with purpose. The purpose is to prevent him from getting into the habit of escaping or resisting the controlling touches. Unfortunately, the methods I describe are physical and require your time, patience, and will. Why do I say unfortunately? Because it is very difficult for people to impose their will upon a sweet unassuming puppy. However, with the methods I've described, if there is not a firm insistence there will be no progress—just continued resistance.

I do believe it is important to have some knowledge of animal behavior prior to attempting to parent a puppy and help it become an acceptable member of the human family. However, I would say that the extent of that knowledge need not be more complex than the relationship that exists between a mother dog and her offspring and the relationship that exists between siblings. If we have some understanding of the fundamental relationships that make up a family, we have a good chance of having success parenting a puppy so that he may become a trusting and respectful family member void of behavior problems.

Often, and especially with older adopted dogs, people are quick to assume a dog has been abused if he has some behavior problem. It really doesn't matter if the dog or puppy has been abused or mistreated or neglected, and it serves no useful purpose to dwell on the issue, because there is nothing you can do to change what has already happened. You have no control over previous experience. You can only control what happens now or in the future—if you have the will and take the time.

Another dynamic I often see from owners is their tendency to blame others for the problems they may be having with their dog. Children are most commonly the ones to get blamed. For example, I once had a client whose dog Mugsey was becoming aggressive, and she felt certain the neighborhood children were to blame because they were teasing Mugsey. I asked what the kids were doing to tease Mugsey. She said they walked to school on her side of the street and when they walked by her yard Mugsey growled and barked at them.

She had asked the children to walk on the other side of the street, but they refused. It did not matter that there was a bigger and more ferocious dog in the yard across the street. As far as she was concerned, they were walking to school on her side of the street just to tease Mugsey. Certainly their presence did stimulate poor bored Mugsey.

I wanted to tell the client I thought the children should be able to walk to school on any side of the street they wanted to, and she should keep Mugsey in the house if she could not control him—not to mention the fact that the children showed good judgment by staying as far as possible from the larger more ferocious dog. But I didn't. Instead, I asked the client why she didn't call Mugsey into the house when he was barking and growling. She said she tried to, but he would not come to her when he was excited. I then asked the client why she didn't go get him when he was excited. She said she tried but he would run from her and once she got him cornered he growled and snarled at her. She knew he would never have done such a thing if it were not for those kids teasing him. Because it started with the kids, now any time someone walks by, Mugsey gets aggressive.

And Horses, Too

Again, if you were to search for the strict origin of Mugsey's behavior, anxiousness would be the culprit. Many animals are terribly anxious creatures. Probably no beast is more anxious than the average horse, and they are said to be flight animals. Since they are the prey and not the predator, they escape by running away from any perceived

threat. Horse trainers have learned to use this flight instinct to their advantage. When I was a child, I can remember my grandfather teaching his horses to face him when
they were approached in a stall. He always said the rear
end of a horse was the business end and did not like them
turning their rear toward him as he approached.

He taught the horses to face him by applying pressure to their rear end, and when they would face him he
would stop the pressure. Pressure was in the form of
tossing a halter and rope toward their rear end. Normally
a horse would run away if you did such a thing. However,
the horse would be in a twelve-by-twelve stall and had no
place to go. When he "faced up," the pressure would stop
and the horse would relax. Eventually, all that was
needed to get the horse to face the pressure was to
merely shake the halter.

More recently horsemen use this principle to teach
people how to work with their horses in a way that is said
to be very natural. They call themselves natural horsemen
or some are referred to as "horse whisperers." They put on
clinics all over the country and help people understand
horse behavior.

These natural horsemen use the horse's instinct to
escape pressure to teach them that the most comfortable place is next to the trainer. A round pen is used to
prevent the horse from escaping. When pressure is
applied, the horse runs in an effort to escape the pressure. However, since he is in a round pen he can't

escape; he can only run in circles. If the horse makes any attempt to face the pressure, he gets immediate relief. In the case of a wild horse, one that has never been handled, the pressure is nothing more than a person moving toward the horse (entering his flight zone). In a relative short period of time—twenty to thirty minutes—the trainer can have the "wild horse" following him around like a colt follows his mother or a puppy follows his mother. When a person watches such a performance it seems rather mystic or supernatural; but it really isn't. Anyone can do it if they have the will.

Although dogs are considered predators, they too are very anxious by nature and prefer to escape pressure like the horse. As we have discussed in a number of chapters, if not allowed to escape, dogs can become very aggressive (fight or flight). When animals feel pressure or feel threatened, they become fearful or anxious unless they have been conditioned or habituated to face or yield to the pressure. When a person or an animal learns to yield to or face the perceived threat, they have learned to trust and, as a consequence, learn to control their anxiety.

When I teach people about parenting puppies, I teach them to use a leash and/or their hands to prevent them from escaping the pressure. A leash or your hands act the same as a round pen. They physically prevent the puppy from escaping. If a puppy gets into the habit of escaping and efforts are made to prevent him from doing so, a real panic or anxiety attack can and often does occur.

I feel that it is very important for people to put their puppy on a leash and keep them on a leash when they are inside as well as outside. The leash allows you to habituate your puppy to all kinds of good behavior. It allows you to control your puppy so that he does not get into the habit of ignoring you if you ask him to come to you or if you ask him to stop chewing on your favorite oriental rug.

Many times a puppy will take something the parent wants and run off with it, and the parent tries to catch the puppy and has no success. The puppy is reinforcing his escape behavior. If on the other hand you have a leash attached to the puppy and he takes off, all you have to do is get hold of the end of the leash and call your puppy. If he does not come, you bring him to you by applying pressure to the leash. At first it may be one step at a time but as you persist, he will come to you to get relief from the pressure. He will learn that being close to the parent in a calm manner is the most comfortable place in the world.

If a puppy parent teaches his puppy to come to him no matter what, he will have taught his puppy to trust. I am not talking about the puppy that clings to his parent and attempts to climb all over him when he becomes anxious or feels pressure. In these cases, the puppy has not learned trust; he has learned to use his parent as a security blanket. I am talking about the dog that has the instinct to become very territorial *and* aggressive and learns to control that instinct. I am talking about the dog that has a very strong instinct to chase anything that moves and yet looks to his parent for permission before he takes off after a jogger or a child running to the house crying with a skinned-up knee.

Two of the most important things to teach your dog are to *come* to you no matter what and to *stay* no matter what. Your dog's compliance to these two requests not only can save his life but they can save you many problems.

Every time someone tells me they have a hard time getting their dog to come to them, I like to tell the story about our dogs, Gus and Gabby. They are in the back yard and Pam calls them and calls them again. She gets her jar of treats and they still don't come. She says, "George, would you call the dogs?" I go to the door and call them and they come running, tails wagging. Pam says, "I don't understand." I say, "Don't understand what?" She says, "I know Gus and Gabby love me but they don't always come when I call them." I explain that love has nothing to do with it. I love my mother, but when I was a youngster I did not always come when she called me. She could call and call, but if I was having a big time out in the yard sometimes I would ignore her. I didn't ignore her because I didn't love her; I ignored her because there was no negative consequence for non-compliance. On the other hand, if my dad called me I would be there in a heartbeat. Pam said it was the tone of his voice. I said, that's right, I knew his voice from my mother's voice and if I didn't come when he called he would immediately come and get me. He didn't have to come and get me very many times for me to learn there was an immediate negative consequence if I did not comply. The negative consequence was not so severe; he might get me by the ear or the arm and guide me along. Today I believe they call it "graduated guidance."

This entire book has been about forming a bond with your puppy—a true bond of mutual respect and love. In my opinion, a true bond is formed when your dog focuses on you and is more interested in what you want than in what might stimulate his urges and instincts. Once you teach your puppy to think about what he does, he will focus on you and exercise self-control.

If we teach our puppies the meaning of "no" early in life, they will be better prepared as they mature. They learn to think, and there will be less stress and anxiety throughout their lives and less chance of dysfunctional behavior. Remember, "no" means stop doing what you are doing no matter what it is. Don't say no if you are not able or willing to apply the pressure needed for compliance. Never scold, punish, or threaten your dog—just say NO.

The parenting methods described in this book are not new. In fact, they are as old as Mother Nature herself. The principle of pressure and relief of pressure is very simple and lends itself to common sense application. The application of pressure (negative consequence) and the relief of pressure (positive consequence) is a naturally occurring phenomenon. If people have the will to apply the pressure and develop the skill to give relief from the pressure with appropriate timing, there is no limit to the bond that can be achieved.

Index

A

aggression, mother dog's tolerance of, 16, 17
animal behaviorists, 13, 62
animal breeders, 62, 67, 69, 70, 71, 73, 74, 76, 77, 78
animal psychoanalysts, 80
animals, human familiarity with, 1
anxiety
    and crate training, 91
    and human behavior, 104, 105
    increases as result of escape, 8
    increases with maturity, 38
    natural for puppies, 22, 31
    puppy can learn to control, 6
    result of attempt to impose will, 2
    root of behavior problems, 2, 131
autism, 56, 57

B

babies and dogs, 122
behavior, objectionable, natural to dog, 9
bonding, 13, 54
breed, "best", 75
breeding, 66, 70, 72, 74, 76, 77
breeds, 41, 61, 65, 67, 68, 70, 71, 72, 75, 76, 77, 78,
    92, 102